GODTALK

*Experiences of Humanity's Connections
with a Higher Power*

Enjoy these other books in the Common Sentience series:

AKASHA: *Spiritual Experiences of Accessing the Infinite Intelligence of Our Souls*

ANCESTORS: *Divine Remembrances of Lineage, Relations and Sacred Sites*

ANGELS: *Personal Encounters with Divine Beings of Light*

ANIMALS: *Personal Tales of Encounters with Spirit Animals*

ASCENSION: *Divine Stories of Awakening the Whole and Holy Being Within*

GUIDES: *Mystical Connections to Soul Guides and Divine Teachers*

MEDITATION: *Intimate Experiences with the Divine through Contemplative Practices*

NATURE: *Divine Experiences with Trees, Plants, Stones and Landscapes*

SHAMANISM: *Personal Quests of Communion with Nature and Creation*

SIGNS: *Sacred Encounters with Pathways, Turning Points, and Divine Guideposts*

SOUND: *Profound Experiences with Chanting, Toning, Music and Healing Frequencies*

WITCH: *Divine Alignments with the Primordial Energies of Magick and Cycles of Nature*

Learn more at sacredstories.com.

GODTALK

*Experiences of Humanity's Connections
with a Higher Power*

NEALE DONALD WALSCH

SACRED STORIES
PUBLISHING

Books may be purchased through booksellers or by contacting Sacred Stories Publishing.

GodTalk:
Experiences of Humanity's Connections with a Higher Power

Neale Donald Walsch

Print ISBN: 978-1-958921-27-2
EBook ISBN: 978-1-958921-28-9

Library of Congress Control Number: 2023940327

Published by Sacred Stories Publishing, Fort Lauderdale, FL USA

Printed in China

CONTENTS

PART THREE: PUTTING IT ALL TOGETHER

MEET THE SACRED STORYTELLERS
MEET THE AUTHOR

PART ONE

Understanding GodTalk

Where there is Isness, there God is.

—MEISTER ECKHART

AN UNEXPECTED VISIT

———————o O o———————

*D*on't look now, but God is talking with you.

How do you suppose this book came into your hands at this exact moment in time? Coincidence? Happenstance? Serendipity?

Really? During the very period in your life when you could really use some answers—you genuinely think you came across these words as a coincidence?

I know, I know, it sounds improbable, if not impossible, that God—if there even *is* a God—would decide to talk with you, *personally*, right now. Why would God want to do that?

Let's consider that question within a larger context. What if God is willing to talk to you all the time—and not only to you, but to all of us? Not just the Pope, or some saints and sages, or an occasional spiritual teacher here and there, or even an author now and then. Suppose God engages in direct communication with everyone who seeks a conversation. Or, to put it even more intriguingly, what if God is communicating with all of us all the time, even when we're not actively seeking such a conversation?

Well, here's the news: Both statements are true.

Oh, and yes, there *is* a God. That's also true.

Now the Higher Power might not be what you think it is, if you think it exists at all. You can refer to it in any way that you wish: He, She, Life, Source, Pure Energy, The Primal Essence, The Universe, etc. But God is real, alright. And two-way communication with this very real God can change your life.

"But wait a minute," you might say, insisting on an answer to the earlier question. "I really need to know. Why would this 'God' that you say exists suddenly communicate with me, if I did not seek such a conversation?"

The answer is that you *did*. You might not know or remember that you did or realize how you did—but you did.

Nothing comes to you unless you draw it to you in some way. Welcome events, unwelcome events, anticipated events, totally unexpected events… all of life's occurrences, experiences, conditions, circumstances, situations, incidents, and happenings are things that you have drawn to yourself. The only question is whether you're doing it consciously or unconsciously, actively or passively, intentionally or unintentionally, purposefully or accidentally.

In the present instance, you might have drawn this communication from God unconsciously or passively, but I assure you that it was an energy within you that magnetized the book you are now reading and delivered it to you— whether you believe that or not.

"Okay," you might say. "Let's assume that's possible. But the opening sentence of this book says *God is talking with me*. I might have found an interest in this book but calling it a direct communication from God is another thing entirely. Did you decide that your first book was a conversation with God just because you *said* that it was?"

No.

Fair question, but the answer is no. I had other, far more compelling, concrete, credible, and convincing reasons to decide that my experience was a direct communication with the Divine. And you might feel the same way about this book after you've finished reading it.

Now, for the record, I'm not saying that every word, every sentence, every passage on these pages is coming directly from the highest power in the universe. But I am saying that this book arriving in your life at this exact moment, and the main message it is designed to bring you, *is* a communication from God. It has come to you through what my wonderful friend Dr. Elisabeth Kübler-Ross, a psychiatrist and author for whom I once worked as a personal assistant, used to call "Divine intervention."

This brings us to the question of exactly how God interacts with us. It is my understanding and my experience that God communicates not just with words, but also—and sometimes only—with actions, events, visions, images, fragrances, sounds, ideas, your feelings, your experience, and an endless list of other phenomena in the physical world.

Did you ever have what you felt was a brilliant insight and wonder if it could possibly be true—then look up at the night sky and, at that exact moment, see a shooting star?

Do you think that just *happened*?

Have you ever come to a halt at a stop sign and started up again, only to feel an urgent impulse to lift your foot from the accelerator and slam on the brake pedal for no apparent reason—and then, as you did, watched a car whiz through the intersection in front of you at an insane speed, seemingly out of nowhere?

Do you think it was simply your *good fortune* that you were not involved in a terrible accident?

Have you ever been served a mouth-wateringly scrumptious soufflé as a guest at a friend's home and then, just before inserting your fork, thought to ask your host, "There's no shellfish in this, is there?"—only to find that the answer was, "Um, actually, yes."

Do you think it was *sheer luck* that you avoided being rushed to the hospital with anaphylactic shock because the soufflé contained an ingredient to which you are severely allergic?

I'd had each of those experiences, and I'm sure I'm not the only one who can tell tales of similar encounters with "fate."

Now, to bring us to the present moment: Do you think that this book popped into your awareness, or just dropped into your lap, out of the clear blue sky?

I'm going to suggest that you called it to you, that you *have* yearned at some level for a conversation about the Divine *with* the Divine, and that it is not a fluke, a coincidence, or an accident that a book with God's messages for you on every page "just happened" to show up in your life.

CAN ANYONE TALK WITH GOD?

———————⚬ ○ ⚬———————

I t is interesting that more people than not believe in a Higher Power—and that most people who believe in a Higher Power openly accept that God speaks directly to human beings.

I'm told that social anthropologists have taken surveys in countries around the world in recent years, asking a single question—*Do you believe in a Higher Power?*—and that the results have come back showing eight out of ten people, in virtually every culture, say yes.

And what I observe, let me say again, is that nearly all those people who believe in God accept that God has spoken to humans. There seems to be little question about this.

We have been told that God spoke directly to, and then through, Enoch, and many agree that this is true. We have been told that God spoke directly to, and then through, Moses, and many agree that this is true. We have been told that God spoke directly to, and then through, Zoroaster, and many agree that this is true. We have been told that God spoke directly to, and then through, Jesus, and many agree that this is true. We have been told that God spoke directly to, and then through, Muhammad, and many agree that this is true.

And those who say that they've heard directly from God have not lived only in ancient times. A man named Mirza Husayn-Ali was born on Nov. 12, 1817 in Tehran, Persia (now Iran) and died just eight years before the 20th century began. He later took the name Baha'u'llah and declared that he had received Divine revelations. Out of his experience, the Bahá'í faith was born, which is now practiced by millions around the world.

The list of people who feel they have heard directly from God grows to this very day. I'll share some examples in Part Two of this book. Of course, not everyone who says they have heard directly from God winds up creating a new religion. But in nearly every case, it winds up becoming the basis of a new person. The person who speaks with God is changed forever, especially if they put into practice what God has said to them.

HERESY, INSANITY, OR REALITY?

Now, in addition to the very special and widely noted cases listed above, most folks would agree that any human being can talk to God. Some people call this prayer or supplication or adoration. But not everyone agrees that God *talks back* to humans. Some people call that idea heresy. Some call it insanity.

It is neither. It is reality.

God is talking to all of us, all the time. We have simply labeled God's communications as something else. Women's intuition, a marvelous insight, an epiphany, or even a stroke of genius. We might feel a startling realization or a sudden impulse.

We might say these unexpected thoughts came to us "out of thin air." We can't readily explain them, and it doesn't occur to most of us—or feel comfortable to many of us—to say they are messages from God. We don't wish to be ridiculed or marginalized, so we avoid such pronouncements, even if we think that God whispering to us is, in a sense, *exactly what happened.*

Now you might say: "Hey, hold it here. You said earlier that God engages in direct communication with everyone who seeks a conversation. Now you're saying that God is talking to all of us, all the time. Which is it?"

It's both.

Here's the deal: All of us are seeking a conversation with God all the time. Even those people who don't believe in a Higher Power are doing so.

We're talking about energetics here.

All of *life* is energy. And we, that is all humans—along with everything else...plants, animals, stones, mountains, planets, suns, stars, clouds, winds, insects, you name it—are energy projectors. We are *made* of energy, we are *absorbing* energy, and we are *projecting* energy in every moment.

The yearning for answers to life's biggest mysteries is a projection of our mental, emotional, and spiritual energies of the highest order. So are our inner pleadings when we're trying to find solutions to deeply personal or urgently pressing dilemmas.

We are *calling out* from inside of us to something outside of us. Whether or not we refer to it as "God," that calling is received and responded to immediately.

Even when we're not being faced with a major challenge or a real calamity but are just dealing with minor frustrations and day-to-day challenges, we sigh and earnestly wish for guidance from *somewhere*—if only from inside of us, where we hope that insight, wisdom, or memory of someone else's similar dilemma might reside.

In this way, we *are* seeking to have a conversation with God—if we believe that God exists—or to connect with *some* wellspring of wisdom and clarity in the universe. We are reaching out to some source of more information about our present predicament or quandary than we seem able to put our hands on in the present moment.

I believe that it is in response to this calling that the book you are now reading has found its way to you.

Now, I say that we are talking to God all the time because we yearn for ease, peace, joy, clarity, and love all the time, and we project that longing outward in nearly every moment of life. These are our natural hopes and dreams, the preferences, and desires of our species.

The vibrations of this energy reach into the universe like the ringing of God's doorbell. We might say that we're not actively seeking a conversation with God, but at the very least, most of us prefer and hope for a good day, a good week, a good month, a good year, and a good life. And when God opens the door and asks, "Can I help you?" our hearts and minds make our desires clear, whether we use words or not.

I see that I am beginning to answer the question that opens the next section of this book.

WHY TALK WITH GOD?

There are moments in everyone's life when we just fall to our knees—often figuratively, but sometimes actually—as we find ourselves confronted with the never-ending challenges of simple day-to-day existence in the physical realm.

It is in moments such as these that talking with God can make a huge difference. Such a conversation helps us understand more, bolstering our stamina and renewing our determination. The information we receive revitalizes our spirits in ways that do not just *allow* us to go on, but motivate, encourage, and *inspire* us to go on.

Sometimes, only a message from God can do that. So, it will serve us to remember what I said earlier: God communicates with us not only with words, but with all the phenomena of the physical world. I've mentioned a perfectly timed shooting star and a surprising impulse to "hit the brakes," which can also happen when you're not in your car, but sometimes in your mind. God's message can also appear in a particular book with a title you had never even thought of reading a couple of months or years ago.

So be open to these messages from God, even if you don't believe in God, or you think that God does exist but would never communicate directly with you.

VIEWS, PERSPECTIVES, AND HORIZONS

Our tomorrows change when our energy changes. Remember when I said that energy creates everything?

Okay, okay, maybe I didn't say those exact words, but I should have. I did say that everything that exists is energy in some form, and now I'm saying that because this is true, energy creates everything that is occurring.

Energy affects energy. You can prove this by pouring boiling hot water into ice cold water, or by saying something to your life partner in a particularly loving tone. Energy therefore produces a change of energy in other things.

Change is another word for *creation*. When a thing changes, it is not what it was before. It has, therefore, been recreated.

Now what we call "thought" is also energy. It can be measured. It can often be *felt*. You can feel your own thoughts and even another's thoughts about you—even if they say nothing out loud about what they think of you. Likewise, others can often feel *your* thoughts about you—even if you say nothing out loud about what you think of yourself.

So we know that thoughts are creative. They are productive. They can generate outcomes.

Now if you hold a thought that there is a God—and that God can and does communicate directly with human beings, *including you*—you will likely find yourself talking with God as you go through your days and nights—especially at important moments on your journey. And yes, you may very often hear God talking with you.

The challenge is that our culture does not hold a universal belief that such a thing can happen, and so we are not widely supported in embracing our experience. Many people write off what they hear as a figment of their imagination, wishful thinking, or even self-delusion.

Yet if we reject our society's general skepticism or dubious response to the idea that God talks to us—and I mean directly and personally, *to us individually*—we will no doubt broaden our horizons, enlarge our perspectives, and expand our views of life as a result of hearing what God has had to say—in a million different ways, in thousands of different moments, across hundreds of lifetimes.

People who hear God's messages and *act on them* enlarge not only their perspectives but their *prospectives*. That is, the chances of their future being filled with real joy, personal happiness, individual achievement, valuable contribution to others, and true inner peace will very likely be dramatically increased.

And *that* is the reason to talk with God.

WE NEED TO BE CLEAR ABOUT THIS

When we speak about talking with God and hearing God's messages, it is *vitally* important for us to fully and deeply understand the *true nature of God*. We must be absolutely clear about the only plausible, valid, genuine, accurate, and credible messages that the Divine would send to us. They will follow these rules:

1. God's messages are always in your best interest.
2. God's messages carry positive, loving energy.
3. God would never, *ever* send a message to anyone instructing them to hurt or injure another.

Sadly, people have sometimes suffered delusions, and then harmed or even killed others, saying that God told them to do so. On a broader scale, more wars have been fought on Earth in the name of God, and under the banner of religion, than for any other single reason.

How can humans do those things? Many of us have often thought about this. Yet even the Bible says that God has called upon humans to kill other humans. If you read that book with a calculator in hand and add up the deaths, you will find accounts of God ordering *millions* to be killed, for a variety of reasons.

Can this be true? No.

It *is* true that such directives appear to have been written into the Bible, but it is *not* true that God actually gave those instructions. I believe the authors of those passages were, simply and sadly, deluded.

How can we recognize a real God message? In addition to running it through the three tests above, I further believe that by entering into your own direct interaction with the Divine, you will find out what is true and what is not true. All of humanity will one day come to understand—fully, completely, and accurately—the true nature of the Divine, and why it could never be true that God ever told anyone to end the life of another.

GOD'S MESSAGE TO THE WORLD

The huge television studio lights were on, the microphones were picking up every word, and the cameras were rolling. "Okay, you claim to have talked directly with God, so tell us… what is God's message to the world?"

The speaker was the famous host of one of America's most popular national television morning shows. He was asking me to answer the biggest question of all time.

"Can you bring it down to a sentence or two?" he added. "We have about thirty seconds."

My mind raced. How could I say something in thirty seconds that would capture the essence of what God wants the world to know?

Then, in one quick flash, I heard God's answer in my head. I blinked and made an announcement that surprised even me. "Actually, I can bring it down to five words."

The host raised his eyebrows, telegraphing a nanosecond of disbelief as he deadpanned to the camera: "All right then, ladies and gentlemen, from a man who says he communes with the Divine, here is God's message to the world . . . in five words."

I knew that millions were watching in households around the globe. This was my chance to bring God's most important communication to more people than I'd ever imagined I would, or could, in my lifetime. Looking straight into the lens, I repeated the words I had just been given to share...

"You've got me all wrong."

I later wrote a book titled *God's Message to the World*. Those five words form the subtitle. You might find that text to be interesting reading.

THE TRUE NATURE OF GOD

If we think that God is vindictive, if we believe that God *wants* people to be killed for reasons that are justified, if we hold that God judges, condemns, and punishes us for not doing what God wants, we will create a world in which *we* will be vindictive, in which *we* will *ourselves* allow people to be killed for reasons that we justify. We will judge, condemn, and punish others for not doing what we want.

This is, of course, exactly the kind of world in which we live.

And yes, many of us have wondered: *How can humans do those things?* We have completely missed the fact that *the way we treat others is based on our collective belief about God's behavior with us*—a belief based on writings from thousands of years ago that claim to reveal what God has told to humans who have talked with him.

Wouldn't it seem prudent for us to have our *own* conversations with God, and find out whether anything of those ancient messages might have been lost in the translation, or misunderstood in the first place?

Have you ever played one of those parlor games in which people whisper something in someone's ear, who then whispers it into another's ear, with that person doing the same, until the message has gone all around the room, only to find that what the last person heard is an inaccurate version of what the first person said?

Multiply that effect times thousands of years and millions of ears, and you can imagine why it might be a good idea for you to have your own talk with God.

The last time I did, less than twenty-six months prior to writing this book, I received a message I called "the God solution." I was told that humanity could and would eliminate a massive number of the problems in our world if we simply embraced a new definition of God.

God, I was told, is most accurately defined by two words: *pure love.*

Now when I share this in a group setting, some well-meaning person inevitably raises a hand and says: "Oh, Neale, Neale, Neale... have we been listening for twenty minutes for you to tell us that the great new revelation is that *God is love?* Everybody knows that! Every religion teaches that. Our religions may differ on dogma and doctrine, but no religion denies that God is love!"

It's in that moment, I find myself gently holding up my hand and saying: "Wait a minute. I didn't say 'God is love.' I said God is *pure love.*"

"Okay," my friend in the audience will respond, "What's the difference?"

"The difference," I offer, "is that *pure love* needs, expects, requires, and demands nothing in return."

Now if we accept this as our new definition of God—and especially if we share it with others, something we'll talk more about later in this book—we will soon realize that this is hugely different from most orthodox teachings about a higher power. It's such an enormous divergence that it raises the question: *Can our species dare to believe it?* To do so would create nothing less than a global theological revolution.

Most world religions would say that it was blasphemy to declare that God needs nothing, demands nothing, and therefore never judges, condemns, or punishes—because they teach exactly the opposite.

But consider this. A new definition would reverse our fundamental understanding of God. It would place a new standard before the world, a new ethic, a new moral foundation undergirding both our collective and individual choices and decisions. We could no longer internally rationalize or justify any less than kind treatment of others, based on our assertion that this is the way God treats us.

I have often observed with despair that many of us can't interact with the person on the pillow next to us with *pure love*. How many of us can swear that when we say, "I love you" to a life partner, we mean "I need, expect, and require nothing in return?" And we certainly can't imagine a God who interacts this way with us.

THE BEST REASON OF ALL

So we see that there are at least three reasons to talk with God:

1. To broaden our horizons and enhance our perspective;
2. To become very clear on the *true nature* of Divinity;
3. To bring *pure love* into our most intimate relationships.

And wait. I can think of another reason, perhaps the best reason of all, on a personal level.

4. To end our loneliness.

I have not yet met a person who has not, at least once in their life, felt desolate and lonely, even with people all around them. Sometimes, *especially* with people all around them.

All of us yearn for someone to talk with about the most important things. Our biggest fears. Our deepest longings. Our worst mistakes. Our biggest regrets. Our most selfish dreams. Our highest hopes.

All of us ache for someone to hear our most agonizing confessions, to answer life's most perplexing questions, and to help us heal our most painful wounds. We need someone to offer us heart-filling, mind-comforting, soul-opening companionship on this long and lonely journey through life.

During those middle-of-the-night realizations, we uncover our fourth, and best, response to the question: *Why talk with God?* And, interestingly, ending our loneliness is what many of us do when talking with God—whether we call it "conversations with God" or not.

Then, there's only one question left.

IS GOD LISTENING?

———◦ ○ ◦———

*G*od is never *not* listening to you. And there is a very good explanation for why this is true.

God is listening to you *all* the time because God is never separate from you.

Let me put this in five words: You and God are one.

All things are *one thing*. There is only one thing, and all things are part of the one thing *that is*. There is no separation between you and God.

Now this again is a deviation from the doctrine of most major religions. The largest number of humanity's faith traditions would call the claim that you and God are one absolute heresy.

God, these religions declare, *created* us, but is not the *same* as us. On this point I agree. Yet affirming that God and you are one is not a pronouncement that God and you are the same.

Your relationship with God is akin to the relationship of a wave to the ocean. The wave is not something *other* than the ocean, nor is it *separate* from the ocean—yet it is clearly not *identical* to the ocean.

The wave is an arising *of* the ocean—an individual oceanic manifestation, if you please—and when its expression is complete, it recedes back *into* the ocean, whence it came.

The ocean is never not *within* the wave. Yet the ocean is one thing, and the wave is another, even though both of them are water. In other words, they manifest as a shared substance, but in vastly different proportions.

In the same way, you arise *from* the Divine, and express *as* the Divine in individuated form, then recede back *into* the Divine, whence you came, to arise and express again in another way on another day.

You are not the sum total of the Divine. The sum total of the Divine is one thing, and you are another. Yet you are made up of the same thing.

God calls that thing *pure love*.

GOD'S LISTENING IS BUILT IN

The reason God is listening to you is not because the yearning you have felt for some clarity in your life is so compelling, or because of God's compassion for you as you face a difficult situation. God is listening to you for the same reason you are listening to the sounds around you while you're reading this book.

Unless you're entering into a meditation, you don't usually sit down in a room somewhere and say to yourself, "I think I'll listen to the sounds around me." The sounds are around you, and your listening is a *given* because of where you are. It is also a given that God is listening to you, because of where *God* is. So you never have to ask, "Is God listening?"

God hears, receives, and understands immediately every thought, emotion, question, plea, or energetic projection you express. How can She be any other way? He's right there inside of you, in the "room of your life," as the basis and the deepest part of *who you are*.

In this sense, God's listening is *built into* the sentient being you call "you," and the process you call "life." God is also listening to you because God *wants* to. That's why the presence of God's essence was created as a "built in" aspect of life in the first place.

Nothing that exists does not contain this essential essence. It is the originating energy, the prime source. And the greatest joy of the Divine is to provide loving guidance, deep insight, expanded awareness, and access to all the knowledge and wisdom that allows us to embrace and experience our *true identity*.

Even as a flower turns to the sun to receive its nourishment, so are we invited to turn to God for ours.

THE WAYS GOD SPEAKS TO YOU

———○ O ○———

have mentioned here that God talks with humans not only with words—
actually, least often with words—but by using every tool of life in the
physical realm. God's messages include what we often call "signs" as well
as feelings, thoughts, impulses, inspirations, insights, sound, visions… and
just about any other device or approach you can imagine.

And speaking of what you can imagine, I asked very directly in my own
conversation with God: "How do I know this is really a communication with
you, and not just my imagination?"

I remember the energy of the response I immediately received. I felt
the sensation of a gentle chuckle, then heard the words: *What would be the
difference?*

*Do you not think I would use any tool at my disposal, including your
imagination, to get through to you? Where do you think Mozart's music came
from? Where do you think the images Michelangelo painted on the ceiling of the
Sistine Chapel originated?*

It has been made very clear to me that just because you imagined
something, does not mean it is not real. It simply means you received an

image of something that may not have been thought of by many others before. It might be something very real indeed, and it often is.

The dictionary defines "imagination" as "the faculty or action of forming new ideas, images, or concepts of external objects not present to the senses." The second definition under that heading tells us that "imagination" is "the ability of the mind to be creative and resourceful."

The external object not present to our senses in this case is what we have called "God," and the new idea we are forming is the idea that not only can we talk to God, but that God can and does talk to us. If this is not an example of "the ability of the mind to be creative and resourceful," then I don't know what is.

So we see that if a person has experienced the ability to form new ideas, images, or concepts about God, this does not automatically indicate that their new idea, image, or concept is delusional. Many are "new ideas" that might have seemed implausible at first but turned out to have been simply an advanced announcement of the actual fact of the matter, shockingly ahead of its time.

May I give you an example?

It took the Roman Catholic Church centuries to admit that Galileo Galilei was right when he declared, in the year 1615, that our planet was not the center of the universe. The Sun did not revolve around the Earth, as the church taught, but rather it was the other way around: The Earth revolved around the Sun.

At the time, his assertion was considered not merely implausible, but blasphemous. Galileo turned more than a few heads around with his announcement. Officials of the Catholic Church were not just surprised, they were annoyed and offended. They declared that his announcement violated the church's teachings, and he was ex-communicated and publicly shamed.

Galileo was, of course, later proven to be right. The Catholic Church as an institution formally apologized—in 1992.

You read that right. I didn't say 1692, I said 1992.

This kind of belated contrition often appears when humanity finally comes to its senses on a particular subject—or you might say, when humanity comes to its *sentience*.

Going back to our dictionary, we see that *sentience* is defined as "the ability to perceive or feel things." Galileo perceived the truth about the Earth's place in relationship to the cosmos. Many people today are perceiving the truth about the place of humanity in relationship to God.

When you feel that God is talking with you, don't be concerned about whether it might be your imagination. It *could* be. Yet that would not mean you are delusional. You might simply be demonstrating "the faculty or action of forming new ideas, images, or concepts" about God.

It is perhaps time we all did exactly that.

WHY WORDS LEAST OFTEN

Since we are exploring the idea that God communicates with us, and the ways in which this is done, you might have caught something I said three times now and wondered about it.

I'm referring to my statement that God talks with humans not only with words—actually, I said God talks *least often* with words, using every tool of life in the physical realm instead.

"Why does God communicate least often with words?" you might ask. "Wouldn't using words make it easier for God to get an important message to us, rather than using an impulse or a sign? Why would God choose to communicate through a feeling, a thought, or an experience, all of which we then must interpret? Wouldn't simple words be a more reliable form of communication?"

Good questions. I wish I had thought of them.

It turns out that, contrary to what one might believe, words are the *least* reliable form of communication because they are open to interpretation and very often misunderstood. And why is that? Well, let me share a bit of information directly from my own conversation with God.

It is, I was told, because of what words *are*. Words are merely utterances: *noises* that *stand for* feelings, thoughts, and experiences. They are symbols. Signs. Insignias. They are not truth. They are not the real thing.

Words can help us to understand something, but experience allows us to know. There are things we cannot directly experience, so we have been given other tools of knowing: our thoughts and feelings.

Now the supreme irony here is that most humans have placed so much importance on the *word of God* and so little on the *experience.*

DON'T MISS A SINGLE MESSAGE

In my own life, I have arrived at a place where I take note of almost *everything.* That includes, for sure, my feelings. It also includes random thoughts, fleeting ideas, and even fragrances and sounds of which I'm suddenly aware. And it includes, especially, my in-the-moment *experience.*

If I hadn't listened to my inner experience, I would never have moved my foot to the brake pedal just as I was about to cross that intersection, I told you about. I would have ignored what I was experiencing inwardly at that stop sign and driven right into the path of certain disaster.

If I hadn't paid attention to the feeling in my heart when I saw that shooting star at the precise moment I described earlier, I would have ignored the insight that caused me to send the notes of my conversations with God to a publisher—and that decision led to a book that wound up being read by millions of people, in thirty-seven languages. That book helped many people recreate their lives in a positive and powerful way.

If I hadn't responded to the gentle prodding from within to ask my hostess if the soufflé she'd graciously prepared contained shellfish, I might not even be here to discuss this with you.

By the way, that's not an exaggeration. I've gone through anaphylactic shock. It can occur minutes after exposure to an allergen. When it does, blood pressure drops suddenly, and then the blood has trouble circulating. The throat swells, airways narrow, breathing becomes labored or even impossible. In severe cases, untreated anaphylaxis can lead to death within half an hour. Fortunately, when I experienced this, I was quickly taken to a hospital which was, as life had ordained it, just blocks away. Doctors immediately gave me an injection of adrenaline, and when I could breathe normally again, I heard one of them say: "That's the last time you'll be eating shellfish, right?"

So yes, you bet, I take note of my feelings, thoughts, impulses, hunches, and the hundred different ways that I know God will use to get my attention. I mean, She will stop at nothing. The ten-syllable sales pitch on a billboard around the next curve of the freeway… the chance utterance of strangers overheard in the coffee shop… the next song that plays on the radio… the fragrance of someone's perfume in a department store that reminds me of something—or someone—I should not be forgetting… all of these are God's devices. And God has more.

What are the ways that God talks to us? Hmmm… I think here of Elizabeth Barrett Browning, who could have been speaking for God when she wrote, in Sonnet #43 from a collection of her poetry published in 1850: "How do I love thee? Let me count the ways."

God's countless ways of talking with us are also God's ways of loving us. So look around you every day and pay attention to all that comes across your path. Listen to the whispers in your ear. Read the words that "just happen" to find a place before your eyes. Use your discernment to see the "signs" that show themselves to you in many ways.

Embrace every positive energy that you feel. Honor every positive thought that arises within you and act on every positive impulse that calls to you.

Act wisely, not foolishly, yes... but don't ignore those messages. Don't set them aside and allow them to be forgotten items on the shelf of your life. And don't let them go unheeded because you're afraid you may not succeed at something God has inspired, or because a message from God seems "too good to be true."

I once actually said this to God in one of my casual exchanges with Him. I said, "Sometimes it's hard to believe some of the things you tell me, because they're almost too good to be true." And you know what She said in return?

"Well, if *God* can't be too good to be true, *who can?*"

So if you have felt God telling you how wonderful you are, how powerful you are, how caring and sensitive and thoughtful you are, how talented you are, and what a gift you are to others... If God has described what joys your tomorrows will bring when you share with the world your inspirations, your personal energies, and your individual creations... don't do what I have done in the past. Don't dismiss God's messages because they sound *too good to be true.*

They *are* true. And when I learned this, when I accepted this and embraced these messages from God to me, my whole life changed. I'd like to tell you more about that, so you can see how God's most uplifting and encouraging messages to *you*, about *you*, can change your life as well.

If there's a part of you that is still not sure God talks with you directly, I'd like you to also hear the personal stories of others who have shared *their* experiences of God talking to *them.*

So let's move into Part Two of this book, which has found its way to your eyes. I'll share stories I think you'll find interesting. Let's see if you agree.

PART TWO

Experiences of Humanity's Connections with a Higher Power

The best dancers know
what grace
every
stumble
contains

—EM CLAIRE

BETTER THAN LILACS

Spring is usually a happy time for me. It had always been during my childhood in the '50s in the Midwest of the United States. The cold winters of Milwaukee finally began giving way to a trace of oh-so-welcome warmth in late March. By April, the seemingly endless chill had become a thing of the past for another year.

In Wisconsin, it was true that "April showers bring May flowers." I remember being overjoyed when our backyard lilac bush began to bloom. I was intoxicated by its fragrance; I'd stick my nose right into the bush, deeply inhaling its sweet smell.

It wasn't hard for me to get into the habit of expecting to feel uplifted in the weeks before summer every year. I observed other people, all over the world, experiencing the same energy shift. There could hardly be anything more natural, as the average temperature increased, the sun stayed out longer, and everyone's favorite flowers came to life. Spring seemed to mean new beginnings in the air for nearly everyone.

But in the Spring of 1992, I was no longer a child with a glad heart. All of us go through bleak periods in life—whether for days, weeks, months, or years—and my downturn was no more significant than anyone else's. But it was serious. I would describe myself at forty-nine as being utterly unhappy personally, professionally, and emotionally. And during what I hoped would be a renewing, refreshing time of that year, my life was feeling like a failure on all levels—and I was angry about it.

Now, my father taught me how to handle aggravation. He said that, whenever I had a bone to pick with anyone important in my life, I should resist the temptation to engage in a verbal exchange with them about what was making me angry. Instead, I should put it all in a letter and then set the letter aside for twenty-four hours. After reading it a day later, if it still felt like a good idea to me to lay my feelings out there in all the words I had used, I should get the letter into the other person's hands.

Dad knew that I would rarely, if ever, choose to say everything I had put in the letter, and that I would never send it.

I'm telling you all this because during the Spring of '92, I did have a bone to pick with a *very* important figure in my life. So I grabbed a yellow legal pad at 4:23 one morning, after a restless night, and I began pouring out my feelings in a very angry letter to God. It was a spiteful, passionate letter, full of confusion and angry questions.

Why wasn't my life working? What would it take to *get* it to work? Why could I not find happiness in relationships? Was the experience of adequate money going to elude me forever? Finally—and most emphatically—*What had I done to deserve a life of such continuing struggle?*

I remember thinking: *"Tell me the rules!* I'll play... I promise, I'll play... *but you gotta give me the rules.* And after you give 'em to me, *don't change them.* Because every other day, the rules seem to be changing around here!"

To my surprise, as I wrote out the last of my bitter, unanswerable questions and prepared to toss my pen aside, my hand remained poised over the paper, as if held there by some invisible force. Abruptly, the pen began moving *on its own.* I had no idea what I was about to write, but an idea seemed to be coming, so I decided to flow with it. Out came. . .

Do you really want an answer
to all these questions, or are you
just venting?

In the first instant, it felt as though I'd actually heard the question, as if there was someone else in the room. I quickly glanced over my right shoulder and, of course, there was no one there. So I just sat for a moment, looking at the words I had just written.

Now I want to make something clear. This did not feel to me like an experience of what some have called "automatic writing." You know… when people say they felt as if another being was controlling their hand.

For me, the fact that the pen I'd been holding began to move on its own did not seem remarkable or even unusual. I'd encountered the same experience on more than one prior occasion in my life—particularly if I had been agitated or frustrated and, following my father's wise advice, decided to "write out" my agitation just to get it off my chest.

At such times, I might find myself frozen for a bit, knowing that I sure did want to write that note to the person with whom I was upset, but not knowing exactly… I mean, *word for word*… what I wanted to say, or the best way to say it.

In such a moment, I'd often seen the writing just start by itself, with something like: "Jim, I think you and I need to get clear about something." Then, with the opening words having come out of nowhere—in a sense, having written themselves—I would consciously and deliberately finish composing the note. I would not call those first words "automatic writing."

I've also had occasions in my life when I knew I owed someone a letter, but I had no idea what I wanted to express. I would take out a pen—this was back in the days when most of us were still handwriting things—and sit there for a minute. Then I'd see the pen begin moving on its own, producing something like: "Dear Mom… I know I should have written sooner." Suddenly, my mind would kick in and I would consciously call up specific thoughts *because* the letter had *already started writing itself.*

I've always imagined these kinds of things to be fairly common human experiences. This no doubt explains the nonchalant way I described, in my first book, my opening encounter with what I now know to be the source of wonderful wisdom and absolute clarity residing within all of us, which I have come to understand is God.

I now also know that my writing in longhand what I was hearing in my head was a purely mechanical response to my desire to remember exactly what came to me in those moments. And I had the feeling that I was not "writing" something so much as "taking dictation," with no larger purpose in mind other than capturing what was being said to me as part of an unusual inner exchange.

What I did not offer, in the opening narrative of my first book, is where the idea seemed to be coming *from.* I had found myself unnerved by what I'd experienced. Instead, I wrote only that an idea "seemed to be coming."

I never imagined, of course, that my earliest legal pad scribblings would one day be read by millions of people as part of a globally bestselling book. I felt that I was engaged in a personal and private process—something that no one else would ever know about.

I DARED GOD

Then why did I send my notes to a publisher? Ah, I've been asked this question many times. I did so because I was told to, in the conversation itself: *You will make of this dialogue a book, and you will render My words accessible to many people. It is part of your work.*

I thought to myself that sending my book to a publisher would be the only way to confirm, in the outward world, the veracity of what my inward world was presenting to me. I held the idea that there was no way any publisher was going to have a team edit, design, print, bind, and distribute a book in which some totally unheard-of person claimed to be having a conversation with God. It was just not going to happen.

And so, I was daring God to prove me wrong.

God did.

These days, I call the dialogue "inspired writing." But inspired writing and automatic writing do not feel like the same thing to me. They do not carry the same connotation or nuance, as I observe it.

Okay... with that clarified, let me now get back to the narrative of my experience in that moment when I wrote: "Do you really want an answer to all these questions, or are you just venting?"

Staring at the words on my yellow legal pad, my mind blurted out a response. I wrote that down, too, scrawling: "Both! I'm venting, sure, but if these questions have answers, I'd sure as hell like to hear them!"

Instantly, I received a reply. This time, I knew for sure that I was hearing it inside my head.

You are 'sure as hell'. . .about a lot
of things. But wouldn't it be nice
to be sure as Heaven?

Now I was at a crossroad between irrationality, irritation, and curiosity. I found myself angrily scratching out: "What is *that* supposed to mean?"

Before I knew it, I was involved in an on-paper dialogue. It went on for three-and-a-half years, although I had no idea where it was going. The answers to the questions I was putting on paper never came to me until the question was completely written and I'd *put my own thoughts away.*

Often, the responses came faster than I could write and I found myself scribbling to keep up. When I became confused, or when I lost the feeling that the words were coming from somewhere else, I put the pen down and walked away from the dialogue until I felt *inspired*—sorry, that's the only word which truly fits—to return to the yellow legal pad and start transcribing again.

Some of the words above came out of the first of the nine *Conversations with God* books, in which I offered my best description of how all of this happened. Here's one thing I know for sure: I am not the only person who has had such an experience.

I often remember fondly an email I received shortly after the first book came out. It said: "There is a lie on the cover of your book."

I couldn't imagine what that could be, so I wrote back immediately, asking what she meant. Her reply was succinct.

"It says, under the title: 'An Uncommon Dialogue.' But there's nothing uncommon about it. It happens to me all the time."

The reader was right, of course. It's happening to everyone all the time—just as it says in the dialogue itself:

I talk to everyone. All the time.
The question is not, to whom
do I talk, but who listens?

It was the publisher who created that subtitle and I didn't see it until the book came out. When I did, I never gave it a second thought. But since then, I've been told by many, many people that they, too, have had similar experiences. And a few others have shared that the *Conversations with God* books encouraged them to reach out to God in the same way, and with wonderful results.

I'm clear that I have not *caused* others to have a dialogue with God, but I may have helped them to know that they *could*, and I am just humbly grateful to have been allowed to be part of that larger process. I know now that this, *of course*, was the purpose of my notes being accepted for publication in the first place.

This has been better than all the lilacs in all the Springs of my life. I now feel *grateful* for the events and circumstances that made the Spring of 1992 seem, at the time, not so sweet. And it is gratitude for *all* the moments of my life that has put a spring in my step for nearly thirty years.

Neale Donald Walsch

GOD'S LAST CALL

"*T*urn right. Turn right! Turn right… right now!"

It was late spring, and we were cruising down the highway while visiting a friend on the north shore of Oahu in the Hawaiian Islands. Tim was behind the wheel, and I was riding shotgun when an unexpected surge of energy rose from my gut, filled my lungs, and flowed into my throat. The words flew out of my mouth with such force, my friend immediately pulled the car over.

Although he could not feel what I was feeling, Tim was a spiritual brother and knew me well enough to know that if I receive a mystical message, it was best to pay attention.

This totally unanticipated detour brought us to a parking lot adjacent to the ocean. Between us and the beach was a small patch of green grass that looked like a small cemetery. Perpendicular to us, about two blocks away, stood a grandiose white temple of The Church of Jesus Christ of Latter-day Saints.

With potent energy still churning in my gut, I hopped out of the car and scanned the perimeter, trying to figure out what might have called us to this spot. Thankfully, Tim trusted me enough to follow my lead.

As we traversed the green grass of the oceanside park, I felt drawn to a small gate that opened to the beach below. I clambered down the stairs, guided by an almost magnetic pull. I let my body pull me to the right. Tim trailed silently a few steps behind.

That was when I felt—and then a second later, saw—a brilliant light slightly above the horizon. It was not the sun; it was midday, and the sun was directly overhead. This powerful beam seemed to pulsate, emitting an energy as intense as the sun.

The force of the light was both irresistible and overwhelming. I felt strongly drawn toward it, even though it hurt to look at it. Hovering just above the ocean, its brilliant beauty drew me in, and yet, at the same time, its painful intensity repelled me. I could not look away from this extraordinary energy source!

Mesmerized, I kept moving along the beach at a slow but steady clip until my body gave out. I could not handle the magnitude of the energy. My legs buckled beneath me, and my knees fell to the sand. Tim rushed over and positioned his body as a haven to support me.

Leaning safely into Tim's arms, I had the security I needed to fully absorb this experience. My body shook as tears streamed down my face. The light had elicited a euphoria in me unlike anything I had ever experienced. Even as my body convulsed with sobs, I couldn't take my eyes off the blinding beam.

Every cell in my body was ignited by the energy. Something about the light felt like *home* to me. I felt I could be absorbed into that brilliance; in fact, I desperately wanted to be engulfed by the energy. I did not want this moment to end.

As I struggled to keep my eyes open to the beauty and ecstasy before me, I heard a deep voice, low and clear, deliver a powerful message: *You're going to want to be sober for this!*

This booming voice stunned me with its clarity and authority. I nodded my head to acknowledge that I had heard and understood. The voice said nothing more and a few moments later, the light faded. My body jerked back to reality, as if the opposing team in a tug-of-war had released their end of the rope. I leaned back further against Tim, gripped with inexplicable sadness that the experience was over.

Tim and I rested on the sand simply breathing in and out together as he waited for me to speak. How could I explain what had just happened? How could I help my friend understand that I had been transported from this earthly plane into what felt like another dimension… and that God had served me up a plate of ecstasy wrapped in the most beautiful bright white light I had ever seen?

How could I make sense of—let alone share—the incomparable euphoria I had felt, and the relevance of the directive God had delivered in a booming, unfamiliar voice?

Luckily, I did not have to say a word. Tim just let me bask in the afterglow. He knew I had experienced something life-altering and that it would take time for my mortal self to process it. He helped me to my feet and supported me as we made our way back to the car. I felt both weary and energized. Perhaps this was how Moses felt after he experienced God's presence in the burning bush.

The intensity subsided, but the message remains with me always.

You're going to want to be sober for this!

Okay, then.

Whatever 'this' might be, I thought to myself, *I will do my best to show up stone-cold sober.*

Although I had occasionally abused alcohol in my younger days, I'd never had a serious drinking problem. Like many people who grow up in Irish Catholic families, I had a love-hate relationship with alcohol. I loved it during celebrations such as weddings and birthdays. I hated when the people I loved drank too much, because it made them disappear from the present moment and, hence, from themselves … and from me.

But if alcohol was a hindrance to my chosen spiritual path of being 100 percent present to the full breadth and depth of waking up, I welcomed this Divine guidance telling me to face the future fully sober. I had witnessed too many people sleepwalking through life, and I did not want to be one of them.

With the inner work that I had done over the years, this Divine message felt both clear and personal. That was why I nodded my head in understanding when the Godly message came through for me. *You're going to want to be sober for this.*

It was not just about alcohol. It was about every way in which I was "asleep at the wheel" of my life, choosing to numb emotional pain through alcohol, food, binge-watching TV, or social media scrolling. I knew that this message was about emotional sobriety, a reminder that these vices might sedate my pain temporarily, but they also made me feel disconnected—from God, my higher self, my truest essence, and my home.

The powerful message I received on the beach in Hawaii has never left me. Nor has the memory of how it was delivered.

Would I ever have the courage to speak of it? Would I someday write about it? Perhaps "coming out of the closet" about this mystical experience would be the next step in my own awakening.

Perhaps this message was meant to be shared with the world.

Emily Hine

A BRIEF OBSERVATION FROM NEALE...

I believe the presence of the Divine is constant and ubiquitous, yet I concede that this may not always be apparent. God does not always show up in ways that we would find it difficult to argue with. Life can surprise us. Divinity's presence can *become* apparent in unexpected, unforgettable, and miraculous events that *assure* us of God's presence.

Such moments can turn out to be among the greatest "presents" of life, bringing with them powerful messages that touch us for the remainder of our days on Earth. This wonderful sharing from Emily offers us a perfect example.

The message here is indelible and, as Emily points out, it is "not just about alcohol." She received a true wake-up call, offering all of us an invitation to push away the daily distractions or attractions that cause us to lose our connection with God.

Never take glorious moments for granted—ours or those described to us by others; and do not shrink from exploring the depths of their larger meaning.

THE TURTLEDOVE AND
THE HAND OF GOD

*a*s I hung up the call from the veterinary clinic, a loud bang startled me and sent my heart racing. A silvery-white bird had violently slammed into my glass door and fallen quickly to her death. An eerie quiet followed.

Turtledoves mate for life. Within seconds, the bird's mate showed up and began walking around her lifeless body as it lay near the edge of the patio. A variety of other birds joined the action, landing in a broad circle as if waiting for confirmation of her demise. It appeared to be a tribute from the bird family.

After a few minutes, one by one, the others began to fly off, leaving the mate alone in his grieving process. The vigil was just beginning. Anxiously, he circled around her lifeless body and then sat beside her patiently, only to get back up and circle again. He would circle, then sit, then circle and sit again. She was not moving. One hour passed. I was totally consumed by the endearing love story that played out before my eyes.

The distraction was nice. I was still procrastinating, avoiding, and lamenting over that phone call.

As I endlessly gazed at the pair, I became part of the turtledove's wake, feeling the surviving bird's sadness. But more importantly, I was amazed by his behavior. I took pictures and videos and stared endlessly at my patio. I went back and forth to another room to look out a different window and get a better view. I was right there with him. Another hour passed, and then another. I would be late for my appointment.

It was time to say goodbye to my beloved dog of fourteen years. It had been four days since her veterinary appointment and I had finally made the decision, after many long conversations and what-if thinking. Today was the day. My earlier call had confirmed my one p.m. appointment.

But now my heart and attention bounced back and forth between my grief and the turtledove's. *I can do a couple more weeks. I can take care of her*, my mind rationalized as Boo slept quietly beside my chair. My dog was failing and in pain, with multiple health issues. She could barely walk and was no longer eating. Yet I was in denial, not ready to say goodbye.

Time continued to pass, and I was clearly late and avoiding my appointment. I was more comfortable in the bird drama than my own. Four hours into this event, my feathered friend was distraught, but remained devoted to his mate. And as I thought about my love for my little Shih Tzu, Boo, I heard something.

Julie, you want to hospice Boo, but you do not have the situational capacity to do that. It is time to let her go. You have been a dedicated guardian by her side, just like this turtledove, but it's now the end. She knows you love her. It is time.

With that, a red cardinal landed on the concrete step in front of me and walked up to the glass door, as if he were an exclamation mark. I shivered as I watched in disbelief. The turtledove's misfortune had served as a comforting directive from the Divine, and I had received the message loud and clear. It was time to take Boo to the veterinary clinic and say goodbye.

The grieving turtledove stayed more than five hours. He was finally scared off by painters who were measuring our house to give us an estimate. I was sad to see him go.

That evening, I went for a walk, reflecting on the events and feeling my grief. My phone rang. It was my husband, checking in. I put him on speaker phone and continued to walk and cry and talk, sharing the amazing story about the turtledove.

He interrupted me and said, "Did you hear that?"

"What?"

"A cardinal. I just heard a cardinal." My husband is a birdwatcher.

I stopped to glance at the tops of all the trees. I could hear his intriguing, unique song—*but where was he?* Following his call, I finally spotted him at the top of a nearby tree. *Was this the same cardinal that had come up to the step?*

Then I remembered I had not shared that part of the story yet. I told Kevin about my visitor and how he had hopped right up to the glass door. Kevin, who is not a metaphysical kind of guy, surprised me by saying, "A close-up visit from a cardinal is a message that your loved one is alright and will never be forgotten."

This was another "God moment" from the mouth of my husband. This emissary of condolence had been delightfully planted at the perfect time and place.

What a great send off from the co-creative hands of God! I thought. But that was not the end of my story.

My red feathered friend has come back every day for twenty-five days now. He comes right up to my glass door, flits-and-flutters around the back patio, and makes himself at home in my private and peaceful sanctuary. Our conversation has deepened. From my delight at our relationship, I've gleaned remarkable insights and continued guidance about an important project I am working on. The bird has given me direct answers to my most important questions, teaching me so much more about life and myself than about death.

Soon, the orioles began speaking with me, too. Outside my glass doors, an enlivening dialog opened, inspiring my writing like a creative muse, and providing a new spiritual spark to my life and work. The conscious, living universe has become an active, co-evolutionary partner in my work, expressing itself in a presence more intimate and immediate than ever before.

Some magical connection opened for me on that "turtledove day" that has initiated a new level of communion with nature. Creator is communicating more directly—not symbolically—especially through the winged ones in my backyard haven. It feels like a steady, ongoing conversation, demonstrating there is no separation between us and God. I had been clairvoyant, clairaudient, and claircognizant—able to see, hear, and know things beyond my senses—but this experience taught me a brand-new language beyond my normal intuition.

Oriole told me this innate capacity is ancient. It is the primary language of many cultures, and all human beings have the aptitude. We are learning how to develop it with more proficiency now. It is time to slow down, tune-in, listen, and be the sacred conduit of love on Earth, where every experience becomes a magical dance with the universe. Information is everywhere, all the time.

This experience, which began with a turtledove slamming into my glass door, has reinforced that something greater than me exists and is here to support me. It has been a blessing during a transformative time in my life, encouraging me to directly participate in a Divine, co-creative conversation. It captured my attention and curiosity, pulling me out of my contemplative, prayerful norm and drawing me playfully into the garden.

I will forever be grateful to the turtledove who gave her life to wake another.

Dr. Julie Krull

A BRIEF OBSERVATION FROM NEALE...

I cannot imagine anyone who could fail to be deeply touched by this story. Feeling the pain of the dove's loss might lead to the memory of our own losses in life. Julie then opens us to the wisdom of what she might well have called a "cardinal rule" of life: Neither mourn nor miss what is going on right in front of you. Look for its profound purpose in moving you forward in your own evolution.

Sometimes it's in the farewell of a dear companion on this journey. Sometimes, it's the unexpected, almost off-handed, in-the-moment observation of someone close to us. Life is opening us to its most meaningful and powerful truths at every opportunity. It is gifting us with ways to advance our most important understandings of our journey here on Earth.

When life ends (for a person, a pet, or even a wild bird), it reaches the reward of its never-ending and joyous life in the realm of the spiritual, from which all physical life springs and to which it returns. Julie's experience opens the door for us all to look deeply into every daily event as communication from Divinity in all its forms. Her story encourages us to see the blessing folded within each happening—including our blessing of releasing a beloved companion.

JOURNEY TO THE HEART

*M*y plane had just landed after circling Uluru, Central Australia's iconic landmark. This awe-inspiring orange rock rose majestically from the heart of the red desert, laden with untold secrets for those who were willing to listen. It seemed to glow brighter the more I watched. I did not know that the Divine, in one of its many guises, was waiting to speak to me.

Seven other women were with me on this weeklong journey that promised to bring us more love, peace, and harmony in a safe and beautiful environment. I had wanted to explore Australia's outback for some time and was yearning to deepen my experience of self-love. When I heard about this trip, it seemed like the perfect opportunity.

As I stood at the lost baggage counter describing my large and heavy suitcase, I was beginning to understand, at a cellular level, that the Divine was already sending me a message: *Let go of the heavy burdens. They are weighing you down. You no longer need to carry them around as baggage.*

It began to dawn on me that this might not be the week of pleasure I had anticipated. I felt tempted to catch the next flight back—but it was too late.

I sensed Uluru standing close by as silent witness, a partner, and a facilitator, assisting with its powerful energy to help dismantle my old, stuck ways. I could hear it whisper: *Birthing the new requires breaking the old down; only then can you let it go. You may feel abandoned in this moment, but you are not alone. I am here standing right by you. Feel it all, precious girl. Let it go and make room for the new to arrive.*

I sat on a mound of red earth facing that grand, wise mother rock and began to sob. Lifetimes of grief poured out, streaking my cheeks with tears and dust. Uluru watched patiently. I could feel her loving presence. No more words were necessary.

I wept solidly for a few days, but then my tears went dry, like the arid earth beneath my feet. I was in sync with the red center.

But I had no time to stop. We were on a journey with one more place to visit. In the middle of the desert, hours away from Uluru, a watering hole had carved itself into the rocks and formed a deep pond. The water appeared to come from far underground. This oasis was hidden at the end of a long, dusty track where the shade of the desert oaks provided a bit of cool relief from the blistering sun.

I sat quietly on a bench, too exhausted to speak while the group chatted with one another at the water's edge. Their occasional bursts of laughter reminded me how isolated I felt. I yearned to connect with love again. After a few minutes, the others left.

Relieved by the silence and alone with the natural world, I tried to absorb all that was happening. My senses came alive; colors seemed more vivid and sounds louder. Mesmerized, I watched a dragonfly skim across the top of the still water, leaving a trail of tiny ripples as its wings caught the rays of the sun. I followed it as it flew off to my right and up toward the red boulders that hugged the tiny cove until it disappeared into a crevice.

I sensed a loving presence in the rocks overhead. Then I watched as one morphed into a human-like face. A broad nose slowly emerged from the rock's surface, followed by two gentle eyes and thick, generous lips. Its enormous capacity to transmit love overshadowed its form and radiated across the pond, hovering briefly in front of me as it infused my heart. I felt profoundly touched, comforted, and eased as it flowed like warm honey through my body. All the sad memories of the past few days fell away.

In the silence, I could hear love speak: *Rest deeply now. You are safe. I am walking with you wherever you are. I am a tiny seed living inside you. Nourish and nurture me. Be gentle, kind, and patient with yourself so you can remember all that is.*

I am uncertain how long I sat there relishing these sacred moments. I did not want it to stop. Finally, my friend came to take me back to the bus. I pulled myself away reluctantly and took a moment to stand up.

"Where have you been?" she asked me. "Your whole face is glowing, and you have a smile that I haven't seen the whole time you've been here."

But I could not find any words. I was still savoring the moment.

On that day, I realized that change is inevitable, but suffering is a choice. Oh, how they will both beg me to take their hands as we walk an unknown, challenging road. I will take that road—but instead of suffering, I will walk along with that tiny, loving seed inside me that whispers, *Let's do this together, shall we?*

Yaelle Schwarcz

A BRIEF OBSERVATION FROM NEALE...

This sharing from Yaelle reminds us that the voice of God—and yes, even an *appearance* that God will temporarily assume to help us visualize the Divine—can and often will arise out of nowhere. Sometimes it happens in the most *unconventional* ways and places. A face emerging from the wall of a mountainous rock formation? Yes. A voice arising out of nowhere? Yes. A feeling of comfort and ease for no particular reason? Yes.

And a message that we might never have sent to ourselves, but that arises in our awareness as an important realization? Yes, that is possible, too. The experiences related here tell us, in wonderfully clear terms, that we do not have to walk our path alone—ever. We *can* do this thing called "life" together. In fact, we *are* doing it together.

Life contrives to show us this truth, as it did with Yaelle—and now, because of her words, it shows the truth *through* her. I mentioned earlier that it benefits us to never take glorious moments for granted—neither ours nor those described by others. We should never shrink from exploring the depths of their larger meaning.

What larger meaning did I find in Yaelle's tale of communication from the Divine? God is with us always and will stop at nothing to make that clear to us—*including guiding you to read this right now.*

WEAR SKIRTS

I love how funny God is, how direct, unfathomable, yet always accurate.

I was working as a special education coordinator in a non-public school. In our school district, non-public schools were private facilities, but the district paid us to work with students that the regular special ed facilities could not accommodate. In some cases, the students' needs were too great, or their behavior was too violent or unpredictable. Several of our students had already encountered the criminal justice system; many were involved with gangs and the local drug trade.

It was not an easy place to work. The other members of the teaching staff were as guarded and angry as the students. I could not blame them. It took all the strength they could muster just to face these students—most of whom had a designation of "emotional disturbance"—every working day.

The teaching staff was also not used to answering to anyone, since the school had never had a special ed coordinator before. I was new. I was a white woman. My presence interfered with the tenuous balance the staff and students had established. Their unspoken agreement was this: not much learning would happen, but fights and other violence would be kept at a minimum.

I had a mission. I wanted to improve learning outcomes for as many students as I could, but I also sought better conditions for the teaching staff. Neither the students nor the staff wanted my interference.

The school director asked me to lead a staff meeting where I could explain my role, including how I wanted to help them and what it might mean for the students. That event was disastrous. The teachers slouched in their seats, arms crossed, chins thrust out defiantly. Whenever I tried to speak, two of them would start a loud conversation about something irrelevant.

I tried asking questions about what they thought might make their jobs easier. They declined to respond. I presented some new ideas. They started throwing their snacks across the room to each other. When I asked about the "wins" they had experienced with students, one teacher got up and left the room, followed by all the rest in small groups. Finally, only the administrator and I were left in the room.

Naturally, I questioned myself. *What in God's name am I doing here?*

At home that evening, I lay on my bedroom floor, letting my tears drip down the sides of my head to the carpet. I felt humiliated, frustrated, angry, and helpless. But I never felt like quitting. When I was calmer and had eaten a good meal, I laid back on my bedroom floor in the dark wondering what I was supposed to do. How could I help and support both the teachers and students? I thought I had some good ideas about how to reach some of the kids—but now my heart hurt.

I asked God what I could do.

Wear skirts, was the reply.

What the h-e-double-toothpicks?

That was it. Those were the words I received. I knew this message was from God because it was pure, simple, and easy to accomplish. It arrived accompanied by a sense of quiet and peace that inspired my heart. I lay on the floor for a few more minutes, reveling in that sense of peace and profound support. It was as if God was like a mother reaching out a hand to her child. The Divine wanted me to get up off the floor and carry on.

The implication, for which I will forever be grateful, was that *God* valued the work I had chosen to do—even if the people involved did not seem to feel that same.

So, okay. *Wear skirts.* I am not a "skirt person," but at the time, I owned a few. I dragged them out from the back of the closet and laid them out on my bed. Then I rummaged around and found some tops that would work.

Starting the next morning, I wore a skirt to school every day.

The first thing I noticed was that some of the younger students began to call me "Miss," instead of some of the more derogatory names they had called me just days earlier. Maybe they saw me as more of a grandmother figure in my skirts. This was encouraging.

When some of the older students saw the younger ones talking to me, they decided it was safe to trust me. And when the teaching staff saw that I was interacting with the students in conversations, even smiling and joking sometimes, they decided I was not the enemy. After I had been wearing skirts for about two weeks, one of the teachers apologized for his behavior in that infamous staff meeting.

I never really did fit in at that school—but I was not meant to fit in. I was meant to have authentic connections with some of the people there, and I did. I worked there for more than a year and I wore a skirt every day, though I have rarely worn one since.

During that year, I helped in many ways. I took over a class for a while. I wrote an Individualized Education Plan for each student. I met with parents and counselors. I started an independent study program to help students who had a hard time getting to school.

A ninth grader in my independent study program arrived at school one day, out of breath. He said he had jumped off his bus several stops early and had run the rest of the way to school because some kids were bullying him and trying to take his backpack. He told me he would have given them his backpack, but it contained a book, *The Giver* by Lois Lowry.

"I will never give up this book," he declared.

It was the first book he had ever read, and it had been given to him by his teacher—me.

We both cried a little. I could see God working through the forgotten skirts in the back of my closet, His love shining through the threads and into the hearts of the wounded and frightened students in my care.

Sue Bryan, Ph.D.

A BRIEF OBSERVATION FROM NEALE...

For me, the most interesting part of Sue's experience is that the words she received when she asked God for help made no sense. They seemed to have nothing to do with *anything*. This fascinating story reminds us that sometimes the insights we receive when we pray for God's assistance *can appear completely disconnected from the situation at hand*. It might be the chance utterance of a friend we just happen to run into on the street...or the words on the billboard around the next turn on the freeway... or the lyrics of the next song on the car radio. These apparently non-orchestrated inputs might feel off-the-wall and unrelated to our prayer for help.

Yet here is something I found to be true in my life, and what this sharing from Sue confirms for me is happening with others: When we ask God directly for help, it's important to *pay attention to what happens next*. Look closely at everything—and I mean *everything*—that comes your way in the moments that follow a plea to the Divine. Then, don't dismiss out of hand what *has* come your way—because it might be more relevant to meeting a challenge or solving a problem than it seems at first glance.

Sue's experience reminds me that Divinity works in magical ways, Its wonders to perform. Sue simply did as God advised. She put on a skirt, and by trusting what she heard, she skirted what could have been continuingly unhappy and debilitating moments in her work and managed to accomplish her mission of helping others.

REMEMBER YOU HAVE MY HEART

I was experiencing cardiac symptoms. At thirty-nine years old, I was too young for a heart attack—yet I had lived directly across the street from Ground Zero as workers cleared the debris from the buildings felled in the September 11 terrorist attacks. I had gotten sick. Now I was afraid my illness had returned. My doctor asked me to wear a Holter monitor for two weeks to assess my cardiac function.

Responding to an inner call to begin my spiritual path and be of service, I had upended my prior life during the height of my professional career to pursue a master's degree in theology. I felt as though I had leapt off a cliff into an abyss. I was in a fully surrendered state. This new health crisis called all that into question.

My graduate seminary felt more like a mystery school led by modern mystics whose mission was to infuse each student with as many rich, luminous experiences as possible in our relatively short time together. I loved attending there, but now I was scared and confused. *Why am I experiencing heart problems? Does life have yet another spiritual two-by-four with my name on it, and is it about to deliver a second command?*

During this health scare, while in one of my seminary classes, I had a vision. I'd been intensely focused on the lecture when suddenly, my professor's voice went dim, as did all the other sounds in the classroom. The face of Jesus the Christ, Yeshua, completely took over my view.

All I could see was Yeshua, full face, front on, golden in color, undeniably present to all my senses. The world was only Yeshua and me. I felt overcome by Divine love, awe, and unbelievable grace. I wept as I felt fully immersed in otherworldly love, as if a whole different realm and dimension had opened.

Let go, let me in, he beamed into me.

Easily, I surrendered. Yeshua's hands reached into my chest and pulled out my heart—and then gave me his in return. I felt immediately transformed and integrated. It was a profound, unquestionable, and mystifying experience. I sat in an altered state, feeling numb and frozen. I could neither speak, nor could I hear.

Suddenly, I wondered if what just happened had been evident to anyone else. Surprisingly, in a class with other sensitives, no one had seemed to notice.

During the drive back to the hotel with my school sisters, all I could do was stare out the window of our crowded minivan, feeling tears prompted by profound longing. The experience had been a deep merging into love, yet it left me with a feeling of separation and grief. I wanted to be anywhere but this terrestrial space. My school sisters noticed that I was in a tender place, they responded in a beautifully non-invasive and non-questioning way, leaving me with my thoughts and feelings.

The following days as I attended my different classes in this beautiful and sanctuary-like setting, I felt oddly isolated—full and empty in the same breath. I drifted through moments of sensing the Divine presence, unconditional love, and a sublime connection to the ineffable. I suppose this is something we all experience. This is the duality of being in a human form, individuated from God, yet with the inner wisdom that we are created from the Divine realms of all that is.

The remaining days of the course were ripe with new epiphanies, undeniably linked to my heart exchange with Yeshua, which had forged a renewal of courage. The most significant of these was an epiphany I had regarding the *alta major chakra*, which in ancient and esoteric traditions is known as the "Mouth of God/Goddess."

When awakened, the alta major chakra becomes an energetic bridge with the high heart, at the thymus. This connection supports the eventual formation of the *antahkarana*, which is one of the threads of the personality's development to merge with the soul. These deep insights became the topic of my master's thesis while at graduate seminary.

I am forever grateful for the life renewal I received from Yeshua. My physical heart was healed and since that day, whenever I've faced challenges, I hear Yeshua's voice say to me: *Remember, you have my heart.*

Rev. Tiffany Jean Barsotti, Ph.D.

A BRIEF OBSERVATION FROM NEALE...

Tiffany's wonderful story reminds us that, when we ask God for help—or, as in this case, when we yearningly pose a question—we will receive a response. Often, the response will arise within the context of our individual lives.

When I was a journalist and writer through most of my twenties, thirties, and forties, I was accustomed to interviewing others, asking pointed questions, and rapidly recording answers. I am not surprised that my own direct experience of God swirled around an encounter that looked the same way. Tiffany was a student in a theological seminary. It is not at all surprising that her direct experience of God swirled around a powerful, in-the-moment connection with the Divine entity who surely must have been the subject of much of her studies.

The point: The context in which you are expressing your personal life in the physical realm can form a sacred container within you that can hold the awesome reality of the Divine. My awareness now is that God communicates with us by choosing the way we can, and will, most easily relate. Then we might feel, at a new level of intensity, what Tiffany refers to as "the duality of being in a human form, individuated from God, yet with the inner wisdom that we are created from the Divine."

Duality does not mean separation from any part of ultimate reality— in fact, just the opposite. We are dual, which means *both* at the same time: human and Divine. We are, thus, one with all others and with God. God has placed the heart of Divinity in *all* of us. That is the message I receive here.

HE ANSWERED ME

have been praying to God since I was a scared, eight-year-old girl when my mother would rush me off to bed so that my alcoholic father would not hurt me. I prayed to God at age fifteen as I rode back to town in the back of a pickup truck after I was raped. I prayed to God at sixteen when I ran away from home with a girlfriend for a week across state lines.

I prayed when my stepbrother and his wife took their own lives. I prayed when my boyfriend beat me and threatened to "cut me up in little pieces so no one would ever know I was here."

I had many arguments with God when two of my nephews were born with serious medical conditions. I asked God so many questions when a family member killed one of her daughters and injured the other two. God and I had a long talk on my wedding day when I knew I was marrying the wrong man. I have talked endlessly to God through every tragedy and every beautiful moment of my life. Our conversation continued as each of my three boys was born.

My family had raised me to pray to God as much and as often as possible. I counted on God to give me direction. Yet during these huge, tragic, and spectacular moments of my life, I never heard God talking to me. I shared my every thought with God, but I couldn't hear a response. My prayers were one-sided conversations.

After seven years of marriage, my husband moved out of our house. I was sure he would return once he had been away from me and the kids for a while, seeing the error of his ways—but that never happened. We began the process of a divorce. I found myself alone with three boys under the age of four. I was terrified.

This was a new feeling for me. It was so different than when it was only me, I had to protect. Now I had three precious lives counting on me. Day in and day out, I struggled to avoid the mistakes I had seen others make during their divorces. I contemplated each move, keeping every ball in the air, trying to be present in my children's lives while still providing for them.

I sold every piece of anything that had meant something to me so we could get by financially. I tried hard to care for my children without letting them see how difficult it was. With an old vacuum, a mop, and a bucket, I started my own cleaning company. Still, I often could not figure out how to get through each day and keep our home. I was robbing Peter to pay Paul— yet Paul was always broke.

One chilly winter evening, exhausted from cleaning an office for one of my clients, I felt deflated and defeated. As I pushed the mop across the floor and wiped down the mirrors in the bathroom, I tried to hold back a sense of hopelessness I had never felt before. The fight and drive were draining from my body. I had no energy left to haggle with the endless bill collectors or meet the needs of my children. I was failing them. It felt overwhelming.

I made my way out into the cold, misty night and sat in my car, crying, waiting to turn on the engine. I knew I needed to make a choice. The gas tank was empty, and I only had ten dollars in my bank account. I had to decide whether to buy gas, so I could get home to my children, or purchase the diapers my children desperately needed. There was not enough cash for both, and I did not know how to choose.

Tell me what to do, I pleaded with God as I sat in the car arguing with myself. My gut told me to put gas in the car, because I could always make a diaper out of a tee shirt or a hand towel.

I remember the chill I felt in the air and the smell of gas fumes in the car from the empty tank. I tried to console myself and remind myself how many things I had overcome in my life. *This is just one more obstacle.* However, I was not sure I could continue this roller-coaster ride I called my life. *How can I keep going?*

As I pulled into the nearest gas station, I squinted, trying to see through the sleet falling from the dark sky. When I stepped out into the freezing weather, my foot broke through the ice and sank into a puddle. Now I felt completely hopeless.

I looked down at my foot and there, in the puddle of icy mud, I saw something—a ten-dollar bill. I melted back into the seat of my car and sobbed uncontrollably, thanking God for this blessing.

I had no doubt that he was the reason I found the money. Then I finally heard God talk to me from deep within my soul, as clear as a father's voice, full of love. He said, *I've got you; I will always have you.*

I spun my head around, twisting it from side to side insanely, wondering where that man's voice came from, but no one was there. The radio was not on. I was the only car in the parking lot, the only person around. I felt wrapped in a warm blanket of comfort that I had never experienced in my life. I sat shaking from the bitter air of the night, but also trembling in awe.

I had talked with God my whole life, never hearing a response until that moment. I knew then that God had answered me, and He always heard me.

M. J. Stanton

A BRIEF OBSERVATION FROM NEALE...

If we look carefully and continually, we will see that sometimes God communicates with us through what we might call "a minor miracle." Would literally stepping right into the precise amount of money one needs, exactly when one needs it, qualify as a miracle? Um…you think? So my biggest take-away here is that *Yes!* Miracles happen, both large and small.

But do you know what? Earlier in my own life, I missed them. I was not *watching where I was walking.* I was paying far too much attention to where I had been and all I had endured. I focused on the things going on right now that I did not like, too busy to even *think* that my next step might take me to something better—or even produce a miracle.

I have since learned that, as my Dad used to say when I refused to eat broccoli: "Son, you don't know what you're missing." These days, I gobble down all the food of life… even the parts that do not seem too appealing. And I keep moving, refusing to let the appearance of things stop me. M. J.'s story reminds me that I am wise to do so, because tomorrow's miracle may be right at my feet.

This account tells us that not only do miracles occur, but that God speaks to all of us all the time, with the same message in different forms: *I've got you; I will always have you.* He is communicating with us even in our final moment on Earth—or maybe *especially* if it is our final moment on Earth.

THE PACT

*T*he year of the pandemic, the trajectory of my life changed.

I can still hear my own screams and feel my fists beating against my head, begging for it not to be true. I remember the cold waves of shock and the crack of my knees hitting the floor. The words—"Your son has been killed in a head-on collision"—will haunt me forever.

Something changed within my molecular field that day. Everything I believed to be right in the world flipped—and now suddenly, it was irrevocably wrong. Seeing my precious son in a casket lowered into a hole in the ground. The person I had grown in my belly was ripped from this Earth, only to be buried within it. This loss eradicated me to the core of my being. Part of me lay down in the casket with him that day, never wishing to surface.

The year of the pandemic, I lost a foothold on my Divinity. All that was sacred to me had been flung into nothingness. My faith was dead. Nothing seemed safe anymore.

From a young age, I had believed in everything mystical—angels, saints, gods and goddesses, the Holy Spirit, heaven, the universe, and higher beings. All were overlaid on my perception of the world like a glorious piece of gossamer. I had an innate knowingness of soul and spirit, and a special connection with nature. I reveled in the Divine and explored the outer worlds of the cosmic consciousness.

All of this served as a way to communicate with God. I grew to be an Earth angel harpist, an animal whisperer—a conduit for all manner of the Divine.

If asked what was most precious to me, the answer was always my children and my divinity, because the two were intrinsically intertwined. My children were miracles bearing witness to my faith. As such, at each birth, God and I made a pact. God would protect my children and keep them safe from harm—always, always.

On the 21st of August in 2020, that pact was broken.

And on the day my son died, God died.

Lost in grief's gyre, I wafted through the following days in a fugue state of existential dread. My soul felt fragmented from the greater existence. I straddled the outer edge of life's nucleus with one foot in the astral planes and one on terra firma. I was the walking, living dead, and the ghost-of-me followed me around. The interminable heartache drove me to despair. Hour by hour, I cried the words, "My boy, my boy, my boy…"

Begging for a miracle, I conversed with empty spaces attempting to reach my son. I needed to know that he was safe. I did not have to believe in God to know my son went to heaven.

I just needed to believe in heaven.

With each passing day, I sank deeper into the abyss. And then, another unthinkable happened. Nine months after my son's death, I sat opposite my doctor with the same sense of cold shock as she mouthed the words, "It is breast cancer…"

Facing my mortality was an existential crisis. I sank so deep into the abyss that the echoes of a thousand angels would fail to reach me, much less the voice of God. Secretly, I welcomed death as an opportunity to join my son. But I knew he would want me to fight, to give something back to life.

My daughter's words tugged at me: "Mum, I can't lose you, too…"

I had two options—give in to life or give up. I did not know it then, but something greater than me would decide.

As I lay on the operating table counting down with the anesthetic, I asked my son to come to me. I prayed to the God I believed had abandoned me—and to Source, to anything or anyone who would listen. Then everything went blank.

A distant part of me heard voices. "Her heart rate is dropping. Increase oxygen."

I was in the post-anesthesia care unit drifting in and out of consciousness when a portal to another world opened. I found a realm where grief's cacophony fell silent and all that remained was the gentle rhythm of something akin to a heartbeat. A feeling of great love swept through me as hazy frequencies vibrated in my head.

Then my son appeared. When he wrapped his arms around me, I knew this was heaven. It was the heaven we had talked about when he was a child. For the first time since his death, I felt no pain. I wanted to stay with him forever.

A voice broke through the barrier. "Deborah, Deborah… come on, wake up."

I did not want to leave my son. I felt the world wrenching me back as I clutched my son, wanting to stay in the other realm. Then the pain returned. They had won.

"It's okay, you are in recovery…"

Dazed and groggy, I struggled to focus.

More voices: "You had a difficult time. We had trouble rousing you and then you gasped, unable to breathe. We had to administer extra oxygen."

I had no words for them, just tears.

A nurse handed me my pendant, an imprint of my son's fingerprint. "Here, let me put this on for you."

Looking up at her, for the briefest moment, I saw his face—just a flash. I knew I had been in the presence of my son and it had changed me. I had experienced something wondrous that served as a defibrillator to my atrophied heart and soul. I knew I needed to find God again, but I also needed to find *me* again. I needed to go back to a place of living, whole, with both feet on the earth.

I wept bittersweet tears. My son had brought me closer to God. My son was in heaven.

I continued to feel my son's presence throughout my cancer treatment, at my bedside when I cried myself to sleep and at the dawn hour when the currawong visited. I began to spend less time willing my son back into existence, and more time willing myself back into existence.

Three months on, I journeyed to Sydney to visit the cemetery for the anniversary of his death. Lying face down on the blanket of grass where he rested, I pressed my chest to the earth, heart to heart. Eyes closed, breathing into the space below, I willed a connection to my boy. A gust of wind rustled through the trees and blew across my legs.

A voice spoke: *I am always with you, mum. When you hear a heartbeat where none should exist, know that it is mine, keeping time with yours.*

I had heard a heartbeat in the post-anesthesia care unit. Now, lying on this piece of ground made sacred by his body, I heard it again.

Tears streamed as I wailed, "My boy, my boy, my boy."

I wept from a place so deep, it was as if my soul poured itself into the earth. Finally, my grief had a place to be free. I felt a release and a profound shift from within. The threads of the Divine pulled me back and reawakened me to life. From that moment, I began to ascend from the realms of the unsurfaced.

Back home, I took the gentle path as I fumbled my way forward in my new roles: grieving mother, woman battling breast cancer, and soul fighting her way back from the abyss. Many days, the spiny fingers of grief dug deep. Cancer treatment left me weak.

The day after I completed radiation therapy, I rose at dawn, grabbed my harp, and ventured into nature. Beneath the canopy of the forest, I nestled against the trees and curled between their roots, letting the gnarly limbs envelop me. I placed my hands on the crusty bark surfaces and listened.

The forest, burgeoning with life, was the sound of all things sacred and holy. I inhaled and exhaled, breathing the rhythm into my soul and spirit. It was as if all of nature was offering a benediction. In the woods, I felt the presence of God.

As I moved forward, I began to again feel the reach of the mystical and magical. It showed up in the colors of the changing sky, the softness of the morning mist, and the glory of the night's nebula.

I was a solitary morning bird opening her wings to the sun's rays, ready to soar. The trembling clusters of molecules that had always held me within nature's wisdom in the presence of the Almighty began to realign. Filaments from my core extended to the universe and finally, even the ghost-of-me faded.

The Earth shifted beneath me the day my son died, in the year of the pandemic. A part of me died that day too—but another part was reborn. My feet had landed on a different Earth.

Some days, the sharp edges of grief still assail me. I miss him beyond imagining. I will never stop missing him, and that is okay. Grief never ends, but it changes shape. Like a moving river, it finds its way through my veins and into my heart. Sometimes, I count how many times my heart has beat since his time in my belly.

In these moments, I simply hold space for grief to express itself. I walk hand in hand with loss and love. There is no separation. There is no leaving one behind or forsaking one for the other. When I feel the weight of grief,

God and my son tell me to lean into them. They invite me to rest in their breath.

I have known the greatest sorrow, and it wove itself into the fabric of my being. I am the alchemy of how these life traumas unveiled more of me—like a flower shedding its petals, new buds forming, blossoms unfolding, decay, beauty, fragrance. I hear my son's voice on the wind, through the ocean's hum and the song of the currawong.

I am here, mum, he whispers. *Always.*

I am Vilomah, a warrior. I was the collateral damage in the wake of my precious son's death, but I survived the ravages of breast cancer. I resurrected from my own "death."

I now know God did not leave me, and I never left God. We searched together, and the journey led back to me.

God did not break our pact. God keeps my son safe in Heaven.

Deborah K. Bates

A BRIEF OBSERVATION FROM NEALE...

I am struck by the clarity and the intensity of the message I receive through Deborah's sharing here. That message for me is that God speaks to us not only in God's own voice, but in and through the voices of others—especially those we love and whose words we trust. It is possible that when God wants to make *sure* we totally get, and truly embrace, a particular message, He may choose to speak to us through the voice of a parent, a child, or a life partner who has gone to the spiritual realm before us. God knows that would be a communication we could not dismiss.

The sharing of Deborah's experience here brings us all an important, life-changing piece of information. This might be something we have always known, have wondered about, or have completely dismissed. That piece of information? Death does not exist. The idea that when our physical body ceases to function, our entire self also ceases to exist—is fiction. It has nothing to do with ultimate reality.

To the soul, death is merely a change of address. Or, as it was put in *Conversations with God*, "a process of re-identification." This is what God helped Deborah, and all of us, to confirm through the announcements from her son.

MOTHER GAIA AND THE GAS GAUGE

had driven this Coastal Plain highway from Maryland to the Atlantic shore many times and knew it well. The familiar, half-abandoned hamlets with their endless fields of soybean and corn stretching for miles. The small stands of forests and soft, sandy soils. I passed signs advertising crab restaurants among ocean resort billboards strung along the towns of Easton, Salisbury, and Snow Hill.

It was mid-June of 2012, and I was on my way once again to sleepy Chincoteague Island on the Atlantic Ocean for a retreat. This trip, however, was different.

Close to the mid-point in my four-hour journey, I stopped to fill up my gas tank and resumed zipping along the highway. My gaze regularly went back to the gas gauge to monitor the fuel. As the miles flew by, I was stunned to observe that the gauge needle seemed frozen pointing to "F." Twenty-five miles, then fifty miles, and then more miles passed, but the indicator didn't budge.

My heart sank. *I am going to need car engine repairs. That means another mechanic's bill.* It would strain my already-limited budget.

The gas gauge stayed on full for 110 miles! Then much to my relief, I saw the needle start to dip. For the remainder of the trip, the gauge slowly dropped down as if nothing unusual had just happened. Yet I knew something extraordinary had taken place. It was a clear confirmation to me that the magical realms my life had shifted into were still unfolding.

Two weeks earlier, at the end of May, I had received a call from the head of the Johns Hopkins Emergency Care after a CT scan at one of their clinics.

"There are numerous enlarged lymph nodes in your abdominal area," the doctor said. "You have lymphoma. You will need to find an oncologist and start medical treatment immediately." His voice was kind, yet firm.

My health had felt a little bit off, yet his words shocked and terrified me. What types of radiation or hard-core chemotherapy drugs would the doctors recommend? As soon as the call ended, I collapsed on my bed, sobbing.

The only clarity I had in that moment was that I was still determined to go to northern Pennsylvania in four days. An Algonquin medicine man was expecting me to join him in ceremony there, and I would show up—regardless of the overwhelming diagnosis.

The medicine man had received a specific request from Mother Gaia in early May that he and I perform a ceremony—with and for Her. Just the two of us. He said he had received clear instructions from her as to how it was to be done. I knew he had been communicating closely with Gaia for years and his connection with her was pure.

Despite my sinking despair, nothing was going to stop me from being part of this ceremony.

I had rummaged through the trash behind a florist to collect enough rose petals to fill a garbage bag and then packed a simple cotton dress, a nightgown, and toiletries. Then I headed north from Maryland.

My destination was a tiny town on the edge of a massive state forest in Pennsylvania, close to the New York state line. The medicine man said he chose it because of a dilapidated, closed-down restaurant with a weathered, life-sized statue of a grandmother figure in front of it. The restaurant had been known for their home-made pies "just as Grandma baked them."

The Mother welcomed us.

The next day, we headed down a quiet trail in the state forest until we found a beautiful space for ceremony under some towering, mature trees. We smudged to bless ourselves and then spread the rose petals on the forest floor to create a short, sacred pathway. These were Gaia's instructions.

Just before initiating the ceremony, the medicine man paused to say: "I'm going to be bringing Gaia's energy and consciousness into your energy body, yet I don't know how you will disconnect afterwards."

All I knew to say in the moment was: "My life is to serve Mother, so I'm not concerned about what will happen afterwards." This was my truth.

Many details of the ceremony have been forgotten, but I will always remember the ancient, powerful, feminine voice that boomed into my consciousness at the conclusion of the ceremony. I knew immediately it was Gaia.

If you surrender to me as much as I will ask you to surrender, I will help you heal from the cancer without the doctors, Gaia said.

Without hesitation, I responded, *Yes, I will!*

If surrendering to Mother Gaia meant I could bypass harsh cancer treatments, I was there!

Ten days later, after the gas gauge miracle, I had to call out to Mother to ask her if she was behind the magic happening in my car.

Chuckling, Mother said, *Yes, my daughter. This is so you can trust me and know that I am taking care of you.*

Much to my physician's shock, the lymphoma was healed within the next sixteen months without any medical support.

My conversations with Mother have been ongoing since that early summer ceremony with the Algonquin medicine man. She has kept me busy with many more ceremonies and other projects since then.

My path of full surrender and accompanying adventures continues.

Mare Cromwell

A BRIEF OBSERVATION FROM NEALE...

This is another of those "minor miracles" we talked about earlier: God communicating with us through here-and-now scenarios that defy all odds—but that *do* happen, nevertheless. Whether it's a gas gauge that stays on "full" for 110 miles or a ten-dollar bill that finds its way underfoot; whether it's a cardinal who pays an up-close visit to our window or an imposing rock wall whose form morphs into a face filled with love, these utterly inexplicable events occur. They include Mother Earth herself calling us to a special ceremony and infusing us with her healing energy. These are signs that God will stop at nothing, using any device at hand to send us pure love.

If something completely out-of-the-ordinary, utterly improbable, or seemingly impossible arises in your experience—stop whatever you are doing. Really stop, look, and listen—*for heaven's sake*. Do not make God work hard to get your attention. These stories point to that wisdom repeatedly. *Pay attention.*

Conversations with God told us there is no such thing as a coincidence. Nothing—read that *nothing*—happens by chance.

ANSWER TO MY PRAYER

The expression on the surgeon's face was strained and urgent. Something was wrong. I could scarcely breathe.

My seven-year-old daughter Erin and I were at an outpatient surgery center, hoping a simple ear tube replacement would stop her recurring ear infections. Erin had been frightened of going through anesthesia sickness again, but I reassured her that this minor surgery was routine, and the misery would be short-lived. Now the procedure was over, but the doctor looked anxious. What could it mean?

He soon explained that he had found a non-cancerous growth in Erin's ear called a cholesteatoma, which he judged to be at an advanced stage of development. He had cleaned out what he could during the procedure but was unable to remove it all. Now he was concerned that the growth might have entered her brain cavity.

I would need to schedule a CT scan through his office immediately. If the results confirmed his assessment, my little girl would need an immediate more complicated and invasive surgery—and this one might endanger both her brain and a facial nerve. We would have to wait for the scan to get a more detailed prognosis.

I had never heard of cholesteatoma, but the surgeon's intense demeanor indicated that he expected a serious situation. We would have to wait a few days for the first available scan appointment, which left me with too much time to worry. I lived alone with Erin and her ten-year-old brother. Although I did my best to hide my concern from both kids, the next morning, as I tried to concentrate on work and anxiously stared at my computer, my stomach was in knots. I was unable to think about anything else. All I could do was pray for help.

"Please let her be okay! I don't know what to do!"

Suddenly, a vision of Erin appeared before me. With absolute clarity, she said, *Call Master Lin.*

I felt chills throughout my body. *Of course! Brilliant idea!*

Master Lin is a renowned qigong energy healer who just happened to live in my general area. I had heard about his skills a couple of years back at a spiritual retreat. At that time, I had been avidly practicing reiki energy healing, but I was unfamiliar with qigong. Somehow, when I heard his name, I experienced a certain knowing—almost an *instruction*, that he was to be my next teacher. But the time had not been right. I had not thought of him since that day and I'd never mentioned him to Erin.

Would it be possible to see him soon enough to prevent the surgery? It seemed unlikely, but I called immediately. I was amazed to hear a receptionist say, "Master Lin has one appointment available tomorrow, and he would love to see Erin."

The next morning, we made our first trip to the healing center for Erin's session. Master Lin asked for a brief description of the issue and then meditated quietly in front of us. He occasionally made some hand motions with his eyes closed. After ten or fifteen minutes, he said he felt she would be fine, but he suggested two more appointments to make sure it was completely cleared.

I felt relieved and hopeful because of his reputation as a gifted healer, but by no means confident she was out of the woods.

Later that night, Erin's ear drained some icky-looking gunk, and my hopes continued to rise. We went to her CT scan appointment and left anxious to see the results. I almost felt sorry for the poor physician as he reviewed her scan. His face became beet red as he stared at it in disbelief.

He struggled to speak but finally said, "I have absolutely no explanation for what I am seeing here. She has no sign of the cholesteatoma at all. I don't understand! I know what I saw. But it's clear that she does not need surgery."

I was overjoyed. She appeared completely healed!

He continued to scrutinize the scan in bewilderment and to search his mind for an explanation for his presumed error. As he stood there, utterly baffled and muttering in embarrassment at his seeming misdiagnosis, I had to ease his misery. I shared with him that we had taken Erin to a reputed qigong healer and that afterwards, she'd had significant discharge from the ear.

He dismissed my comment completely. "No, obviously I fully cleaned out the growth and was mistaken anything remained." *Sigh.* At least I did my part to plant a seed that energy healing might have something to offer.

More tests confirmed that the growth had indeed been substantial and was present long enough to cause some bone loss. Erin now wears a hearing aid in the classroom but otherwise, she has fully recovered.

Thanks to the clear instructions that came as an answer to a prayer and Master Lin's help, she avoided the more invasive surgery.

Marcia Lowry

A BRIEF OBSERVATION FROM NEALE...

I have observed that repetition is another of God's ways to get our attention. Have you noticed, for instance, that here is another story of God speaking through the voice that we cannot ignore? And it does not have to be the voice of a loved one who has passed before us and is now speaking from the spiritual realm. It could very well be the voice of a spouse, asking us if we heard a cardinal chirping, or the voice of our own seven-year-old child—not heard in real time, but coming to us in a vision not unlike a movie, staged by the Great Director.

I have repeatedly heard the same kinds of experiences from different people, sharing with me at completely different times and places about their communication with the Divine. Each time, I become even more convinced than I ever was of what God said to *me*: "I talk to everyone. All the time. The question is not to whom do I talk, but who listens?"

THE SUPERNATURAL WASHING MACHINE

*H*aving experienced a few happy days in a row, for some reason I woke up feeling out of sorts. As I took my seat for meditation, I took a few breaths and asked the question: "What is this sense of unease and what can I do about it?"

I was not expecting an answer, although a vision and knowing came in very strongly. I was shown a humongous washing machine... about four times the size of a "normal" one. It was front loading and I got the message, *Time to do the wash and deep clean.*

I laughed to myself. I am not a huge laundry fan and I have done so much other clearing and cleansing work in my life. I thought, *Really? A washing machine?*

Images of shirts followed with words written on them that I have said to myself in the past. "I am not worthy." "I am afraid." "I don't know what the next step is." And there were so many more.

The shirts were different colors, and I began to wonder about their significance. I noticed some of them did reflect the chakra colors. I received this message: *These words have stained you as clothes get stained. It is time to rinse them clean.*

Next came the memories. I had an image of my screaming step-grandmother and the "little me" feeling her stress. Usually, her yelling was not directed at me—but her anger always filled the room and it felt threatening. That image of my step-grandmother and myself was on a longer shirt, like a nightgown—clothing that might cover my whole body.

Then came another image of me at an extremely uncomfortable time in my life. It was one of those moments where you look back and think, *Well there were signs for* that *one. I could have avoided that if I had been paying attention and listening.*

With that memory, I could feel my defenses kicking in, and as soon as they began to, another message came: *You are ready for this cleansing. Not just words, but memories can be cleansed away now.*

I repeated the exercise, throwing words and memories into this humongous washing machine. I did feel some emotions as they came up, but I did not let them grab me. I just noticed them and then focused on the fact that they were going to be washed away!

I put a *ton* of detergent in the washer in my mind's eye and slammed that door shut with a loud bang! As I did, I felt sweet relief. I saw myself searching for the "high power" cycle to make sure all was thoroughly cleaned... I did not want *any* stains remaining. I saw the image of everything going around in circles, and I watched as you would in a laundromat. A feeling of peace swept over me. I had support. A deep clearing was going on.

I heard a *ding* in my ears as the washer stopped. *Hang these up to dry. They need the sun to dry them so they will be permanently cleansed.*

Growing up in New York City, I have never hung clothes out to dry, but this mental image was so vivid. I approached a clothesline festooned with clothespins. As I took each article of clothing out, I gave thanks that all of them were blank. None of them had any writing or images on them. I hung each one on the clothesline and watched them bake under the hot sun.

I knew the sun was doing the last part of the cleansing. It was truly allowing "the Light" in after the stains of my own self-talk and past hurts had been cleaned away.

I walked between the lines of clothes, touching them and feeling deeply blessed. Smiling, I gave thanks for the cleansing message I received from the supernatural washing machine.

Jenny Mannion

A BRIEF OBSERVATION FROM NEALE…

This unusual sharing offers an opportunity to make the point that GodTalk is occurring in our lives in a hundred different ways across a thousand moments. Can totally "off-the-wall" thoughts and images that come to us out of thin air be God talking? Absolutely. And when a "vision and knowing," as Jenny described, comes to us strongly—utterly unrelated to anything—it is most likely the Divine using symbolism and metaphors to make a point.

The dictionary defines *metaphor* as "a thing regarded as representative or symbolic of something else, especially something abstract." If Jenny's experience is not an example of that, then I do not know what is.

Yet couldn't such visions and words simply be the workings of our imagination? As you may recall, I addressed this in the first part of this book, describing how I asked God that very question. Do you remember God's reply? *Do you not think I would use any tool at my disposal, including your imagination, to get through to you?*

The message that I find in Jenny's sharing is this: Do not dismiss the meaning of metaphor—"imagined" or not. She embraced the metaphor, without questioning its origin, and it has served her mightily to do so.

God is always communicating with us, using every tool at his disposal—including our creative minds.

THE PRESENCE OF GOD

Years ago, as I walked alone on a cool, spring day, I found myself in the presence of God.

For more than a year, I had planned a sabbatical from my university research and teaching responsibilities. I wanted to learn about a new area of science, and I was simultaneously writing a large grant that would soon be due to the US National Institutes of Health.

A few weeks into this break, I decided to walk alongside a tall hedgerow that had caught my eye the day before. It was just starting to bloom and was surrounded by fresh, fragrant mulch. As I walked, my perception began to unexpectedly and subtly shift. A deep joy swept through me, as did a sense of recognition. I thought, *I have been searching for this my entire life, and here it is!* I was experiencing the presence of the Being who created me and everything that existed. It was as plain as day. For the first time in my life, I understood what Divine love was and learned I could experience it.

The presence was vast, extending for miles in all directions. It was tangible and alive in its own way, yet I could only remotely sense the God at the center emanating the presence. The experience lasted for a few minutes, then faded. My perception returned to normal. But the joy remained, along with a growing sense of awe.

Over the next three weeks, I stepped in and out of this presence. I carried with me a continued sense of anticipation, never knowing if or when it might return. Each time it did, I found I could probe further. I wanted to clearly see the being residing in its center, although I never really did. I saw only vague images in my mind.

I felt a growing sense of purpose, as if things were building towards something. *But what might it be?*

The answer came one morning as I found myself having a different kind of experience with this presence. Whereas before, it was something I encountered but did not really interact with, this time it was paying attention—to me. That day, I heard it communicate clearly: *It is time to surrender and let go of yourself.*

As I began to understand this message, I felt fear. *If I surrender myself, will I still exist?* I wondered. *Who will remain or will my existence cease to be?*

Truthfully, I had no sense of the answers to these questions. These thoughts occurred in a flash. Another part of me acknowledged that if I were to surrender myself, it should be now, while I was in the presence of God, surrounded by this love, light, and absolute caring. The words *Have faith* then came into my mind.

And so, without fully understanding what it meant or what I was doing, *I let go.*

Immediately I felt an expansion and illumination of my awareness. A sense of peacefulness and silence emerged. I quickly realized that "I" hadn't disappeared into oblivion—but this new "I" was different from the person I had thought myself to be all my life. This was the actual me, and I knew I had always been that.

Over the next few hours, the experience of the old me began to fade away. Through my inner eye, I saw that former me as a large ball of dynamic, swirling energy, a collection of thoughts and feelings, a history of experiences. I saw, too, that only a small portion of my perception had been anchored in the present moment. This was how I used to experience things, with part of me associating with past experiences and another part routinely projecting into the future, anticipating coming events. Once I let go of that prior me, the past and future disappeared too. All that remained was the peaceful silence of the present moment. Fortunately, although my connection to the past dissolved, all the memories remained.

In the days that followed, I needed to make some adjustments—and to be honest, some of it was challenging. Within two days, one of my brothers unexpectedly arrived for a visit. Of course, I recognized him and remembered our family history, but I no longer felt the same sense of connection we once shared. He was strangely unfamiliar to me, yet at the same time not. The same held true for my wife at the time, my daughter, and other family members and friends. People and things seemed foreign; nothing was personal as they had once been. Letting go of the prior me had created a void, to be sure. But importantly there was a larger love too, and much deeper.

The love remains dominant, a love for everyone and everything.

Paul J. Mills, Ph.D.

A BRIEF OBSERVATION FROM NEALE...

This remarkable sharing strikingly reinforces the comment that I offered following the entry above, from Emily. There, I described the presence of the Divine as "constant and ubiquitous." This is precisely what Paul tells us he experienced while casually taking a walk one day alongside a just-blooming hedgerow.

Others, too—and you may very well be one of them—have felt this magnificent presence at a random moment or in a random location, neither of which had any special significance in their lives. It is important to never discount these experiences. Never let them pass through you without sticking to you—even though they might, as happened with Paul, change your experience of "you" and of everyone else.

You'll recall that Tiffany Jean referred in her sharing to what she called "the duality of being in a human form, individuated from God, yet with the inner wisdom that we are that essence created from the Divine." Paul's encounters with his brother and other family members and friends mirror this experience.

Yet I would not want the assumption to be made that the Divine presence removes us from our closeness with beloved humans. When we experience Divine love, we can often simultaneously experience a closeness with others *like nothing ever before*. We might feel a less needy kind of attachment that is even more intimate. In the same way, when we feel deeply aware of our oneness with all others, and with God, we might sometimes feel detached from ourselves.

Put into other words: Our relationships become *richer* and *more* meaningful, precisely because our emotional neediness has vanished. We can love others for who they are, without worry or concern about what they will give to us. This pure love is life changing.

ASK HIM

It was almost impossible to drive on that early spring day in Sweden. Despite the flowers already struggling to push their way up through the warm earth, the morning air was still chilly enough to freeze into dense, patchy fog. I could only see about five car-lengths ahead. And as I inched along, I worried that elk might suddenly appear on the road south of Gothenburg.

And I couldn't stop sobbing about my unsalvageable marriage. In my agony, I pleaded aloud, "What can I do?"

Suddenly the fog lifted for a moment, and I saw my answer.

The sign said, "Askim, 13 km." Through my tears, it looked like, "Ask Him." And in my heart, I knew that was what I had to do.

I followed the sign, turned off the road, and saw an outline of a church I knew was there. It was only around three hundred meters away, but I pulled over and tried to collect myself so people would not see me crying my eyes out. And when the car stopped, a beautiful feeling of peace and great love cascaded over me. It felt like being held in someone's arms. I sank into the feeling and realized that it was giving me a calm sense of strength. Eventually, I felt strong enough to step out of the car and walk toward the church.

I had to cross through a cemetery, its gravestones obscured by the dark fog. But this eerie experience did not scare me. I knew it was because of the enormous sense of love and support I felt.

I gently opened the church door so I would not disturb anyone if a service was underway. But the building seemed dark and empty. I made my way up the aisle and sat down on a bench close to the altar, resting for at least a half hour. Little by little, my mind became clearer. The sense of calm grew. It felt so lovely that I wanted to stay in it as long as possible, as I feared that it would vanish if I stood up.

Then I repeated my question from the road: "What can I do?"

The answer came immediately to my mind: *Leave.*

At that moment, a ray of sun pierced the fog and streamed through the colored glass of the church window, illuminating the altar in a golden glow. The painting of Jesus Christ also began to glow. The story of the resurrection came to mind. I knew what I had to do.

In my mind, I said *Please, stay with me.* Then I stood and walked back to the church door.

Just as I was pushing down on the door handle, I heard a key turn and the door swung open. I was taken aback, but the poor church warden looked as if he had seen a ghost.

"How did you get in?" he stuttered.

"The door was open," I replied.

He shook his head. "It is never open outside service hours." He motioned for me to walk out and then, with gusto, firmly locked the door behind me.

It was as if I heard God chuckle above me. My heart got lighter. On the way back through the cemetery, my eyes caught a name on one of the headstones: Sandwall. Immediately, I heard a voice saying, *It is only a wall of sand ahead.*

These words and my experience in the church empowered me with the determination to carry on with my life.

Agustina Thorgilsson

A BRIEF OBSERVATION FROM NEALE...

Well, there could hardly be a better example of God using an improbable scenario to communicate a message than allowing someone in need of an answer to open a *locked church door,* walk right in, sit quietly in a house of God, and get a response in one word. But wait! How about if the Great Director of this scene has the lead actor leave through a cemetery and encounter a message of significance *carved in stone*—and then explains it in an unmistakable voice, so that the meaning could not be missed. Sound unlikely enough?

I have this idea that if we all look back through our own lives, we will find what I call Moments of Improbability that we might not have thought of *then* as a communication from the Divine, but that we see now as *exactly* that, with no bones about it. And more messages might be on their way, by the way, because this *is* one way that God *shows* us the way to get on our way.

I could not, incidentally, find a way to use the word "way" more often in a single sentence.

Sometimes life's unlikely scenario may be sophisticated and complex, with lots of plot twists and turns. Other times, it might be simple—like the way this book made its way to your eyes.

OUR MIRACLE BABY

My husband and I had been married for eight years and we had been trying for a baby since our honeymoon. I had gotten pregnant in the first year of marriage, but I had miscarried that soul after only eight weeks. Then an ultrasound revealed that I had cancer. I was thirty-one. I chose a completely holistic path to wellness and fully recovered from cancer—but despite my strong, healthy body, I had been unable to conceive again.

We had applied for inter-country adoption and had just received notification that all our background checks had been approved. We should have a baby within twelve months. We went to bed that night feeling elated and excited that our long wait for a baby would soon be over.

During the night, a dazzling, golden light woke me. I could feel a warm glow on my face. To my left, hovering over me, was a tall, golden being. The form was human-like but illuminated completely by golden light. The most incredible love emanated from it. It was unlike any love I had ever felt. I could feel my heart burst open as tears streamed down my face.

My whole body began to heat up and I could feel and see rings of golden light moving up and down from the top of my head to beneath my feet. I then felt my body pivot from side to side on the bed and I became aware that, energetically, I was now in a standing position. The waves of light continued to pulse up and down my body and the energy began to intensify.

As the rings of light expanded further out around my body, I could feel a pressure building in my lower abdomen. I then felt a massive release and a long, white, jelly-like substance fell out of me from between my legs onto the floor, where it immediately disintegrated.

Then, for the first time, the golden being spoke. It told me that what had been stopping me from getting pregnant had now left my body. *Rest now, and all will be well.*

The next thing I remember was waking up in tears, shaking my husband awake so I could tell him what had happened. He said that he had slept soundly and was unaware of anything. "It must have been a dream," he suggested.

But I knew it was not just any dream. I had never experienced anything like this before. I still felt different, somehow lighter and brighter. I jumped out of bed and could not wait to phone my sister and tell her about my incredible experience.

Six weeks later, I was getting ready to travel on a short flight for my annual scan at the cancer unit. The night before my trip, I was aware of gentle vibrations moving through and around my body. I felt very calm and at peace, which was unusual for me, as I was always apprehensive for a few days before I had that scan, afraid of what the doctors might find. This time, I didn't feel that way. I did a pregnancy test that night, just to be on the safe side, because I knew I was going to have several tests and scans at the hospital. The pregnancy test was negative.

I did not think any more about it and the next day, I made my way to the airport. The whole journey went smoothly. I had to wait two hours before my appointments, and for some reason, I was drawn to visit a cathedral close to the hospital. I had worked just across the road from this beautiful cathedral for years but had never visited it before. I went inside and sat in a pew at the front and closed my eyes to pray. Immediately, I could feel a beautiful energy like an angel behind me, wrapping its wings around me in an embrace. A warm glow surrounded my body. I was in a state of pure bliss.

Another visitor startled me by touching my arm. "You must have fallen asleep," the gentleman said. "I was afraid you were going to fall off the seat!"

I looked at my watch and saw almost two hours had passed. I had to rush to make my appointment at the hospital.

My doctor was happy with what he saw on my scans. I would have to wait for some blood tests to come back, but everything looked good. I was elated with this news as I made my way to my next appointment.

At the dental surgery, my dentist wanted to take an x-ray. "Is there any chance you could be pregnant?"

I said, "I don't think so. I did a test last night and it was negative."

The dentist, who had known me for years, said, "Well, I would feel happier if you went to the pharmacy next door and get a pregnancy test you can take before we do the x-ray."

I did the test in the restroom at the dental surgery. You can only imagine my joy when the result was positive! My whole body vibrated with excitement as I called my husband to tell him the news. I wanted him to know before I told the dentist. My husband was obviously over the moon.

I went on to have a strong, healthy pregnancy and we were blessed with a beautiful, healthy baby boy. Two years later, we had a beautiful baby girl! Miracles do happen.

Siobhan Maguire

A BRIEF OBSERVATION FROM NEALE...

Siobhan describes, in excellent detail, what the actual moments when she was experiencing her connection with the Divine were like. Our experiences will not all be identical, but the specificity of this description can be helpful to others, who might otherwise be wondering what in the world is going on if they encounter some of the same unusual bodily phenomena.

I remember how, at the outset of my own conversation with God, tears flowed down my face as a warm glow encased my heart. I had no idea why that was happening, but I let myself be okay with it, just as Siobhan tells us in her experiences.

And this happened in a church ...though she didn't have to go through a locked door to get in! All of which brings up something my mother said to me when I was a child: "Honey, wherever I am is my church. God is everywhere." It took me forty years to experience that as my truth as well. I hope it has not been, or will not be, that long for you.

THE LITTLE WHITE OWL

*W*e had just left our friend's farmhouse that September night and were meandering along the rural road with the car windows down, so the warm night air could caress our faces as we traveled home.

As we crested the highest hill, the Harvest Moon was in full view and its sheer magnitude made me gasp. Its pale orange glow seemed sacred, as if the moon itself was manifesting God.

But there was something in the road up ahead.

My husband and I stopped just short of it and leapt from the car, rushing to see what it was. The white object, illuminated by the light of the moon, was the body of a small bird.

To my dismay, I recognized it as a juvenile male barn owl, its heart-shaped, white face encircled with golden-brown feathers, its eyes closed as though in a deep, restful slumber. The little owl was perfect in form with its long, rounded white wings tucked closely by its sides; the white underbelly feathers were flawless, pure white with a hint of gold mixed in, and its short, white tail extended a few inches below the body. There were no signs of trauma and no indication of how this baby owl had met its fate.

My husband and I looked at each other with deep sadness, and without speaking, I gently scooped up the lifeless little bird, cradling it in both hands. I felt the velvety smoothness of its feathers and the warmth of its body, all signs indicating that only a short time had passed since the little bird's life had ended.

I quickly surveyed the surrounding countryside, and my eyes came to rest on a hay barn across the road amidst a vast open field of freshly cut hay. The rich, spicy fragrance of the newly harvested hay reminded me of the complex, earthy aroma emitted by a vintage bottle of Pinot Noir.

The barn, with its weathered clapboard and gable roof, might have been the little owl's roosting site during the day. Once evening fell, he would have swooped out over the open countryside, flying low over the freshly cut field of hay, looking and listening for small rodents scurrying about. But this little one would fly no more.

My husband opened the rear door on the driver's side and placed a piece of cloth on the floorboards. I tenderly laid the little bird on the cloth making sure it was nestled in and closed the door. I returned to the driver's seat and noticed the car's clock read 11:11, a number that had become a special sign for me, typically a precursor to spiritual phenomena. I wondered what message was awaiting me.

On the somber drive home, we decided to bury the owlet in our backyard, in an area where we had previously interred our beloved pets. I had recently purchased an antique wooden box at a flea market; we agreed this could be its coffin. My husband offered to dig the small grave.

But when we opened the back car door, the cloth lay empty; the little white owl was gone!

How could this be? Had the bird somehow recovered and managed to wiggle himself under one of the seats? My husband grabbed the flashlight from the glovebox and we searched under both front seats, and then throughout the entire car, but there was no sign of the owl. We looked at each other and shook our heads in disbelief.

Another thought occurred to me. "Maybe he regained consciousness just as I was closing the rear door, and he somehow managed to fly out unnoticed."

"We can go back and see if he's there," I said.

We returned to the spot where we had found the owl, and there it was, lying in the middle of the road in exactly the same spot! It was as though we had never stopped to pick him up the first time, except we were traveling in the opposite direction.

Once again, I gathered up the bird's body and laid him on the rear floor on the small cloth. I felt like we were in a version of the Twilight Zone. How was this possible? We both knew we hadn't imagined it! I could remember how the little bird had felt in my hands, warm and soft. I thought I had seen my husband looking over his shoulder at the bird on the original drive home. There was no doubt the owl had been in my hands and in my car—and then had vanished—only to reappear in the very spot where we had first encountered him!

In an eerie *déjà vu* trance, we once again pulled into our driveway. This time when I opened the rear door, the white owl lay motionless on the cloth. We resumed our previous burial plan in dumbfounded silence.

Lying in bed that night I could not stop thinking about what had occurred. What kind of message was I supposed to get from this event? That reality is not at all what I thought? That matter and mass were nothing more than an illusion?

I thought about the stories my mother, who was of Native American descent, had told me as a child. The white owl symbolized inner wisdom; change and transformation; intuitive development and self-actualization. In her stories, the white owl's animal spirit acted as a messenger, carrying wisdom from the Great Spirit. Anyone fortunate enough to encounter a white owl, she had said, would receive the gift of communication with Great Spirit by inspired written words or intuitive channeling. The warm childhood memories flooded my mind as I fell into a deep sleep and began dreaming.

I looked up at the overhead canopy of looming pines. The massive trees had shed only a fraction of their greenery in preparation for the coming winter months and the discarded needles created a thick carpet of fragrant pine needles underneath my feet. Nightfall was approaching as I heard the raspy *whoo-whoo* of an owl in the distance. I quickened my pace until I could see the magnificent bird perched on the low-hanging limb of a splendid pine tree.

The white owl looked directly at me, opened its beak, and said "Listen to me!"

I sat straight up in bed, struggling to become fully awake. I quickly pulled the chain on the tableside lamp and reached for my notepad and pen. After I had jotted down as many details as I could remember of my dream owl encounter, I turned off the light and went back to sleep.

The following morning, I took the pad in hand and read the words, "Listen to me!" What was I supposed to hear? My dream had abruptly ended just as I got the command to listen. I had the same dream again on the next two nights. Each time, I woke up just as the white owl spoke.

Having long been interested in the practice of inspirational writing, I was motivated to give it a try to understand what message the owl had for me on the night of the Harvest Moon. I tried a few times, but I was unable to quiet my mind enough to write. So I decided to stop trying to force a message. I would wait until I felt inspired.

A few days later, that inspiration came as I sat on my back deck and watched a downy, white feather float by. It drifted back and forth, back and forth, riding a current in the warm air, finally landing at my feet. I immediately knew this was the sign I had been waiting for.

I hurried inside, grabbed the nearest pen and paper, and began to write.

Pamela D. Nance

A BRIEF OBSERVATION FROM NEALE...

We have perhaps now become accustomed to hearing of improbable or impossible scenarios—a ten-dollar bill in the mud, opening a locked church door, or a brilliant light appearing out of nowhere on the horizon—that I trust you need no further convincing about how the Divine uses unlikely and inexplicable real-life events to create unreal circumstances that drive a message home.

Do not, therefore, be surprised if a white owl appears in your own life, acting... just as Pamela's mom said they do... as a messenger carrying wisdom from the Great Spirit. It might simply be a white feather finding its way to you—or, as I suggested earlier, a most unusual book that places itself before your eyes. The author tells us that the white owl symbolizes inner wisdom; change and transformation; intuitive development and self-actualization. Is it possible that a mesmerizing *story* about a white owl could do the same?

Maybe this is the sign that *you* need. Grab the nearest pen and paper and begin to write. Create a record of what is flowing to you, and through you, in this moment. It could be important. It might be meaningful.

It could be the Divine, talking to *you*.

THAT IS THE HEALING

The pain was incredible, and so discouraging. My symptoms indicated a flare-up of Crohn's disease. At age twenty-three, I was out of remission from this incurable disease… again.

I had been dealing with Crohn's for more than ten years and I had nearly died several times. Facing the pain or yet another bout left me sad and scared.

I knew that this time, what lay ahead was worse. In the past, doctors would give me medication that helped for a while; when I reached the point where medication was no longer working, a surgeon would remove a section of my diseased bowel. This would relieve my symptoms for a few months, but then the disease recurred, and we went through the medication and surgery cycle again.

This time, I was out of spare parts. If medication could not get my symptoms under control now, I faced an ileostomy: the surgeon would remove my entire colon and bring the end of my small intestine outside my abdomen. All my digestive waste would go into a little bag attached to that opening. I would have to empty the bag myself, by hand. The idea was horrifying to me.

I was scared to be sick again, with pain and persistent vomiting draining my energy. I didn't know if I could go through that again. And what about my *life?* Where was the fun, the joy, the discovery most of my peers in their early twenties were experiencing?

I had wonderful doctors, and they did their best. They really cared, but they could not help me find a permanent cure. Round and round I went in a debilitating cycle.

At that time, in that part of the country, I had few options. Even chiropractors were considered quacks. No alternative healers offered services nearby. And this was before the internet, so there was no easy way to research what to do.

About the same time that I received this news, I heard that a friend was in the hospital. She had fallen in the shower and hit her head. The most recent report said things were looking better and doctors expected her to recover.

On a warm, humid night in July, a little after ten p.m., as I lay in bed reading, trying to distract myself from my worries, my mind was suddenly filled with light and was cleared of all thought. I saw my friend's face drifting by and I knew that she had just died. A silent voice, an impression of thought, told me it had been her choice. She was twenty-seven years old. She left three small children behind.

The voice also told me that I had a choice. If I did not take my health into my own hands, I would be dead before I reached twenty-seven—in less than four years.

As the light faded from my mind, I grappled with what I had just experienced. The episode had not been frightening, but the message had scary implications. I knew it was God talking to me. It had felt so powerful and unusual.

I was stunned and saddened that my friend had died, and the message about my own health was clear. I had to take my health into my own hands.

But what did that mean? What if I was unsuccessful? If the doctors did not know what to do, how could I possibly figure it out?

If I were wrong, would I die?

Whenever any kind of crisis came up in my family, we prayed. It's just what we did. When I had been in the hospital through the years, prayer chains had formed all over the country. It was natural for me to turn to prayer when something happened that I did not know how to deal with.

I got up the next morning determined to spend a lot of time in prayer. I did not know where to begin taking my health into my own hands, so I decided I would ask God what I needed to do. I vowed to spend time in prayer each morning and each night. And I would ask God for a healing. When I prayed, I would feel the healing energy of God surrounding my body, sinking into every cell.

The stakes were high. I wanted a miracle this time: total healing. I believed in miracles. I knew *anything* was possible, and therefore it was possible for me to heal, even from something incurable. While I waited for a flash of light or something dramatic, I would take the medication doctors were recommending. That way, I felt, I was doing everything I could for my body.

I kept my vow and spent time in prayer twice or more a day. Something unusual began to happen; I started getting answers. I had experienced the power of forgiveness before; now I felt guided to forgive everyone and everything. I reviewed my short past and made lists of anyone I had ill will toward, as well as all the experiences for which I needed to forgive myself. I used prayer and visualization to help me forgive.

The mind-body connection was not very widely known back in those days, but I learned about it and really believed it. My emotional life needed attention if I were to reach a healthier level of stress.

Days and weeks went on. I learned to meditate. I changed my diet. I exercised. I did not get the big flash-of-light healing that I was waiting for, but I felt a little better. When I looked back later, I realized that God was guiding me, step by step.

Inspired, I created a collage of pictures of healthy, athletic people and I started each day looking at the photos and imagining the feeling of being well and strong. My doctor and I developed a healthy partnership.

Then things got interesting. Books that held answers for me came into my life; they fell off the shelf at the library or bookstore. I overheard conversations that had important pieces of information for me.

I read an article that said, "No matter how far down the path of illness you have gone, you can heal." That was quite a radical thought! One sentence jumped out at me: "If you have denied yourself a wish, a dream, or a desire, you have to go back and give that to yourself."

As I turned within, I realized that there were many things I had denied myself. I joined a "record" club and started broadening my exposure to music. I loved to sing but did not do it much, and never in front of anyone else. Although I loved listening to other peoples' music, I knew there was music inside of me that I longed to express. Now I wanted to play an instrument. I had tried before, even though I could not read music.

Inspired by the article and dedicated to reclaiming my health, I went back and slowly re-taught myself some songs on the piano. That made me happy. I taught myself guitar and eventually started writing songs. I had always wanted to drum, so I learned some basics.

I was already an accomplished nature photographer, but now that I was expanding and discovering new parts of myself, I felt a stronger sense of beauty than ever before. I started to bring beautiful things into my space and to nurture myself with them. I loved color, so I surrounded myself with it.

I had always been fascinated by acting, but an early school incident had traumatized me. Now I revisited that dream, forgiving the teacher involved. I auditioned and was cast in my first play as an adult. I loved it!

My love of drawing had also been a casualty in school. During this healing period, I picked up a pencil and started to draw again.

So much of what I had denied myself was my creative expression. Over the months, it became obvious to me that I had a great deal of creative energy to channel and enjoy. I did not know it yet, but I was an artist!

My intuition developed and I realized that I was quite psychic.

Every morning and evening, I continued to pray. I looked forward to visualizing the well-being of God around and within me. About six months after I started this process, I knew I was in remission. With my doctor's help, I began to wean myself off the medication.

I felt good! Maybe I did not feel totally healed, but I was much, much better. Still, I was confused. Where was my miracle healing?

One day I got angry at God and yelled, "I've showed up every day for six months, expecting to be healed!"

Of course, all this time I had been expecting a miracle in the moment, like a big flash of light indicating without a doubt that I was healed. It had not happened. What was going on?

And in that instant, light once again filled my mind and my inner chatter ceased. I heard the words: *If you had been healed in a flash of light, you would have recreated the illness. You needed to change. That is the healing.*

With that, my mind and body filled with peace.

Crohn's disease has not recurred.

Anne Cederberg

A BRIEF OBSERVATION FROM NEALE...

This sharing from Anne brings us an intriguing piece of information not found in any of the other experiences we've heard about here: When we pay attention and give energy to what brings us joy and opens us to our creativity—singing, acting, playing piano, drumming, photography, woodworking, gardening, or producing culinary delicacies—we shift the energy within us, projecting *creativity itself*. Creativity can spill over into other areas of our experience and help us create positive outcomes and solutions to life problems.

This shines a focused light on the mind/body connection, which is a part of our journey here on Earth. That connection can play a big role in our collaboration and communication with the Divine. When the mind and body are expressing as one, they are standing in the doorway to the Divine.

Add the power of prayer, which Anne employed with purpose and intention, and the soul joins the mind and body in communion with God. It is not surprising to me that her physical healing followed.

FROM TERROR TO TRUST

When the facilitators at the personal growth workshop asked me what I hoped to gain from the weekend, I knew that answer. I desperately wanted to release my fear.

I was afraid of what other people might think and do. I avoided conflict. Losing a relationship terrified me. I feared being different and making a fool of myself. People had betrayed me so many times that I was afraid to trust.

Most of all, I was afraid of my fear.

The facilitators asked us to make four commitments: do not chew gum, don't interrupt, be on time, and do whatever we were told.

I had no problem with the first three requests, as I never chewed gum and did not often speak in front of strangers. Being punctual mattered to me. But that last requirement …

History had taught me that humans had ordered other humans to rape, pillage, steal, and kill. I was conflicted. I truly wanted to learn how to release my fear, but I did not want to promise I would obey.

Still, I was afraid of being different and losing the workshop I had paid to attend—so reluctantly, I said yes.

My decision nagged me all week as I waited for the second weekend of the workshop to begin. I knew the facilitators would demand the same four commitments again. Was I going to cave in again and agree? I decided: *No, I will not.*

But this was scary.

Through the sleepless nights ahead, I worried about this decision. What would the facilitators say? How would the other participants act? How should I prepare? My what-ifs tormented me.

Fortunately, I had spent several years in Nar-Anon, a support group for families and friends of addicts. Nar-Anon had taught me that the only person I could fix was myself, and that I needed the help of a power greater than myself. Nar-Anon would have suggested that I "let go and let God."

I did not like that word, "God." I had always considered myself an intellectual agnostic. "God" made me think of an old man with a long, white beard, sitting on a thundercloud with a lightning bolt in his hand, waiting to strike me dead if I failed to obey some rule I didn't even understand.

I did like the words "power greater than myself"—but whatever that was, it hadn't helped me deal with my terror. I felt I could not do this by myself, and I did not have time to engage in the niceties of semantics.

One night, I threw myself to my knees on my living room floor and pleaded, "God help me!"

Suddenly, a magnificent calm flooded my body.

Somehow, I knew that together, we could do it.

The second workshop began. As I had expected, the facilitators asked us again to make the four commitments. I refused to agree to do whatever they said.

The room turned surly. The facilitators said, "This workshop will not continue until everyone agrees!" Then they walked out, leaving me alone with a furious group of participants.

Everyone argued with my decision. Bill had taken time off from work to attend the workshop. Jane was paying for a babysitter so that she could attend. Raymond slammed his fist on the table. Mary screamed in my face. John called me an "uncooperative bitch." Yet I felt nothing but compassion and love toward them.

The facilitators returned and asked me to leave the workshop, so I did. It no longer mattered. I had received exactly what I had come to receive: the release of my fear.

That workshop experience taught me some valuable consciousness lessons.

First, I became aware that two levels of conflict were happening. Externally, I was dealing with facilitators who demanded I adhere to their rules and with other participants who would become angry if I refused to agree. Internally, I had been in conflict with myself. I could not sleep, my muscles were taut, and my body trembled.

But simply being aware of my external and internal worlds was not enough. I had to make a conscious choice to detach emotionally from the facilitators' control issues and the participants' anger and not allow myself to get sucked into their issues. I had my own terror to deal with, and that was enough.

By making a conscious choice to ask a higher power for help, I brought my mind back to the present moment and to what I needed to fix in myself. I simply chose to trust that a power greater than me could help me, and other traumatized human beings could not.

I realized that, at first, I had focused on my external world and what others might do in the future. But by focusing on others and the future, I was giving away my own power in the present moment. As soon as I started focusing on what I could do right here, right now, I reclaimed my personal power.

When I took my power back and then chose to ask for help from a power greater than myself, my fear disintegrated.

To figure out my next action step, I had to ask myself the right questions: *What do I think? What do I feel? What do I need? How can I get what I need without hurting others?*

In the workshop situation, I had been conflicted. I needed help in releasing my fear, but did not want to ask for it, particularly from God. Yet when I finally asked for help, I immediately got what I needed, without hurting others.

By saying no, I also helped the other participants. They had focused so intently on what I was saying and doing. They were afraid they would lose their valuable time and money. Some exploded in rage. All were trying to control and manipulate me.

A friend later told me they spent the rest of that weekend examining their conduct toward me.

Dr. Janet Smith Warfield

A BRIEF OBSERVATION FROM NEALE…

I think the big lesson in this story—the *enormous* message, if I could be allowed an effusive word—is that, as Janet put it, "making a conscious choice to ask a higher power for help" can be a huge turning point in our personal process as we face life's challenges. It places the energetic emphasis where it will undoubtedly bring us the most benefit, allowing us to—again using Janet's exact words—"trust a power greater than myself," instead of turning that power over to the traumatized human beings around us.

By turning in a different direction when we need help in creating a change, we can produce a shift in our interior emotional environment. Then we can feel peace where there was agitation, assurance where there was anxious hope, and serenity where there was insecurity. And *that* can produce a major change in our exterior reality.

The above account of one person's interaction with God is about more than may meet the eye. Pushing back against people who want to push us around in a personal growth workshop might seem to be among the least of life's challenges. But Janet's sharing is a great reminder of the grandest power in life. It invites us to also reclaim *our* power in *every* situation, by reclaiming our direct access to, and connection with, the higher power of the Divine… which exists within each of us.

When we acquire the confidence, skill, and determination to use that power without hurting others, as Janet qualifies, we empower ourselves to let go of our fears, too. What a fabulous message from the Divine!

LIVING A MIRACLE

*I*n autumn of 2020, I noticed a small swelling on my son's left forearm. I was sure it was just another insect bite, so I applied allergy cream and gave him allergy medicine. When the swelling did not decrease in size, I started to worry.

The pediatrician in our Romanian town advised us to get scans and blood work. The blood tests were normal, but the scans showed inflammation—probably ganglion inflammation, they said. "But you should get a biopsy to be sure that there is nothing more serious."

Biopsy was a serious and scary word. Suddenly, everyone around us seemed to be concerned.

Our second opinion, from a prestigious pediatric hospital in France, was that he had cat scratch disease. *Cat scratch fever?* Yes, that made sense. My son played with cats on the street. But those doctors also recommended a biopsy, to rule out the worst-case scenario. My instincts told me it might be something much worse.

We decided that, while we awaited the biopsy results, we would make our annual visit to family in Florida. The biopsy was traumatic for both of us, leaving a large wound. But we cheered ourselves by looking forward to a trip away from the harsh Romanian winter.

During the flight, my son began to complain of a fever and pain in both legs. When we landed, we took him to the hospital. The emergency room doctors sent him to a nearby pediatric hospital, where they diagnosed stage 4 rhabdomyosarcoma—an aggressive muscle tissue cancer that had spread to his lymph nodes. The prognosis was poor; he had only a 20 to 30 percent survival rate. We received this news on my son's fifth birthday; the next day, surgeons implanted a port, and he had his first chemotherapy treatment.

Everything happened fast. I was devastated. "Why are you doing this to me and to my son?" I demanded of God. "Why are you punishing us?"

I did not hear an answer. I could not listen anyway.

Nothing made sense anymore. My religious beliefs, perceptions, and accomplishments—everything felt useless now. I fed my family organic food. I was a reiki master with a spiritual mentor. I was trying to meet God in so many ways—and now he had gone missing.

The oncologist's treatment plan was intense: fifty-four cycles of chemotherapy, radiation, and surgery plus six months of maintenance treatment. He said an adult could not withstand this regimen for more than four months—and Ayan was just a little boy.

Ayan started the treatment immediately and it was horrible. He longed to go back home to Romania, but we had to continue this brutal regimen to have the best chance to save his life.

Four months later, the tumor was considerably smaller. It was time to remove it surgically.

"Can this surgery heal him?" I asked the surgeon.

"Yes," he said. "It could be cured."

As part of my family's healing journey, we had decided to see every new development as "a wake-up call and not a death sentence." We would change whatever we needed to: even our beliefs, behaviors, values, priorities, and motivations to live.

In May, during Ayan's surgery to remove the residual tumor, surgeons discovered his ulnar nerve had been cut, possibly during the Romanian biopsy. They replaced it with a nerve harvested from his leg and we started occupational therapy sessions to strengthen that arm.

More treatment lay ahead. In September, doctors began radiation sessions in addition to the chemotherapy, which left Ayan in pain and exhausted. Sometimes he needed tube feedings, and he received many blood and platelet transfusions. My husband had returned to Romania, returning to visit us every few months. We still had family support and our brilliant medical team.

We had God in all His forms.

I began training in alternative therapies, such as healing meditations, tapping, shamanic energy medicine, and sound healing. My son was excited to practice with me! I believe these therapies supported his little body as he endured the traditional medical treatments. I felt these healing modalities activated a new connection between me and the Great Spirit, changing me from within.

Finally, we were ready to go back to Romania to be with my husband. We loved our home there, and we had so many plans: we'd redecorate the house and adopt some pets. It was so exciting! We did the last scans, booked the flights, and prepared to leave.

Then the doctor called with alarming news. "Anca, we see something strange in your son's forearm. We need to do a biopsy. We are sorry, but you cannot leave the U.S. yet."

Those words felt like a knife in my heart. I knelt and said to God: "I did everything I knew to support my son's healing journey. Please, just take everything I feel from me, all my heaviness and desperation. Tell me what to do. May your will be done."

A few minutes later, alone in the shower, I heard a voice say, *Take your son to his favorite place and do only what makes you happy, nothing else. When you have negative emotions, hand them over to me. I will take care of them.*

Suddenly, I felt a new energy inside my body. I booked a vacation to the Florida Keys, my son's favorite place. He was so happy. He put his hands on his heart, closed his eyes, and asked God, "Am I healthy? What is inside my forearm that the doctors suspect?"

Then, looking at me, he said, "Mom, there are two spots, but they are not important. I am fine."

I chose to trust him. I was proud of him—but still so scared.

We had a great time in the Keys. Many times each day, I handed over all negative emotions that tried to paralyze my body. I was breathing consciously, inhaling light and exhaling density. Each time I did, I felt calmer.

During this beautiful vacation, we went to the hospital to follow up on my son's forearm and got the news: "This is not a relapse. We were just seeing the grafts of the new nerve that we put there. Ayan, you are good to go back home. We will miss you."

Oh, what a feeling! That moment changed me again. A new transition. A new life.

Before Christmas, we were back home in Romania with our British short hair cat, our parakeets, and a wild hamster, back to living life as the miracle it is.

Anca Radu

A BRIEF OBSERVATION FROM NEALE...

Yes, words will come to your head when you least expect them—while you are in the shower, loading the dishwasher, or cutting the grass. When you are "on automatic," doing mindless things, your mind is out of the way. The space is wide open, the tablet blank, the blackboard empty. Anca's experience is a powerful reminder that these are frequently the moments when the voice of the Divine can be heard the loudest.

For me, there are two messages here! One, *create* such moments, despite the hustle-and-bustle of your day-to-day life. Spend time being "out of your mind" on *purpose*. Take a few moments in the shower, as Anca did, or looking out a window, or taking a walk. Do it two or three times a day. Create the space for God to whisper, and for your soul to amplify what She said. You'll be amazed at the wisdom God will send you.

The second message? When such moments occur without you deliberately creating them—when they simply arise in the natural order of things—*do not go immediately back to what you were doing*. Give yourself the gift of a brief respite. Your mind was not quieted without reason. Your life was not stopped without purpose. God speaks in the space between your thoughts.

When I tell people I have had conversations with God, some of them have said, "Man, are you out of your mind?"

My answer is always: "Yup."

MY ANGEL GEORGE

Many years ago, I attended a physician's workshop to enhance my ability to help empower my cancer patients and speed their recovery. One of the strategies we were taught was guided imagery.

"Close your eyes and visualize what I describe," the leader said.

I had no belief in what he discussed, so I just sat looking at him until he noticed I was not following his directions. Then I closed my eyes to trick him into thinking I was doing what he said. That is when things got interesting.

I am an artist and a visual person, and suddenly, I could see everything we were told to visualize.

"Walk along a path and meet your inner guide," the leader said.

I figured Jesus, Moses, or Maimonides would appear—but instead, a bearded fellow wearing a cap and a white spiritual looking robe appeared—and spoke.

My name is George.

Well, I was disappointed, but I still found it interesting. After that, George would occasionally pop into my mind and speak to me. He would give me directions about my life from what I should wear to how I could handle life-changing events.

One day, as I was about to go to the hospital where my father was dying, George asked me a question. *How did your parents meet?*

I don't know, I thought.

Then ask your mother when you get to the hospital.

I did this and learned that Dad took my mother on their first date because he lost a coin toss! My mother told more humorous stories about Dad, too.

Although he was in a coma, I sensed Dad could hear her regaling me with these tales. He started smiling and looking wonderful.

Maybe he will survive a while longer, I thought. But when the last family member arrived, Dad took his last breath.

After that, I trusted George's advice about everything.

I noticed that my lectures were also more spontaneous. One night, as I was giving a lecture, I stopped paying any attention to my outline and just let the words flow out of me. A woman approached me afterward and said, "I've heard you speak before, and tonight was better than usual."

I agreed with her.

Another woman came up said, "Standing in front of you for the entire lecture was this man so I drew his picture for you."

It was George.

From that night on, I let George do it.

I have learned that George is my lifelong angel. He saved my life when, as a three-year-old, I choked on a toy and nearly died. He helped me when I fell off our roof, and he got me through some terrible car accidents.

Now I conceive of myself as *his* instrument. Just as the TV set portrays the programs but does not create them, I do the talking in this life—but George writes the script.

Bernie Siegel, M.D.

A BRIEF OBSERVATION FROM NEALE...

I love this story because it describes how visualization can be a potent device. Bernie tells us that he saw an angel when he was guided to close his eyes and see himself walking down a path. The power of suggestion is so important here. Bernie was not told to visualize, specifically, an angel, but rather to meet his personal "inner guide." Bernie did the rest by shutting out the exterior world, inviting his mind to step aside, and creating the space for the guidance that was waiting and wanting to show up.

The Divine is in communication with us all the time—literally, in every single moment. The very best way to receive the messages—whatever images, events, and understandings God is inviting us to embrace—is to give ourselves that kind of mental "break." I was just talking about this in my preceding observation.

Be an angel to yourself. Do not miss an opportunity to step into these golden moments—and do not ignore or reject the messages God sends you as "just your imagination." As I have suggested over and over, *pay attention.* When you do this, you no longer need to be "at tension" in your life.

I could, of course, be wrong about all of this. But I don't think so.

THE CHALLENGES NEVER END

*P*art of me imagined—after having nine books of my dialogue with God written, published, and distributed—that "my work," as God described it, was complete. Perhaps you'll understand my surprise, then, when I found myself pulled from a sound sleep at just past four in the morning on August 2, 2016 by an insistent inner feeling that there was more to do.

I didn't know what that could be—but I knew that I had to do *something*. This feeling, the inner call, couldn't be ignored, and I knew that, despite the early hour, there was no way I could lie down and go back to sleep. So I threw back my covers, climbed out of my bed, and trudged into my den. I plunked myself into my chair, opened my laptop, and sat there staring at the screen. I was frozen again in a moment when I knew that something wanted to be written, yet not knowing what.

Oh, I knew I'd be writing again at some point in my near future: a column for *Huffington Post*; a blog for *CWGConnect.com*; a response to a journalist's emailed question. A Facebook entry. An answer to someone posting at my online *Ask Neale* column. Even a full-length book in my voice only, exploring the messages I'd received. Something.

But another on-paper conversation with God? Another back-and-forth dialogue with a deity? I thought those days were over. I thought that process was complete.

I was wrong.

What felt like it was going to be another major colloquy began flowing through me. And sure enough, it wound up being the ninth book in the dialogue series. The publisher called it *Conversations with God—Book 4*, because it was the fourth book carrying the same three-word title as the opening trio of books in the series.

Since that middle-of-the-night moment that brought the book into being, I've come to fully embrace the truth that there's *always* more to be done, no matter what a person's life work is. The challenges in *every* area of life never end. The invitations to do "the work" that the soul came here to do never stop coming.

Just when we think, *How much more can it take to fully awaken?* Life says: *Glad you asked. Take a look at this...*

Then you find yourself facing a major moment when you get to decide who you are and who you choose to be—again.

That is "the work" we are talking about here, of course. It's not really work in the sense of being laborious, but more like the joyous work of doing anything you totally enjoy, as you strive for new levels of excellence.

CAN 'BEST' BE MADE EVEN BETTER?

I've told the story in my previous writing of my Dad and his apple pies. My father made the best apple pies in the country—certainly, the best in our county. But he was not actually a cook. He couldn't make a hamburger without burning it. Yet somehow or other, he found a way to make astonishingly good apple pies.

Whichever way he'd learned it, he knew exactly how to create pies with just the right amount of diced apples, butter, sugar, brown sugar, cinnamon, nutmeg, and lemon juice, all wrapped in a pie crust so light in its flaky goodness that it almost fell off the fork.

My father made those incredible apple pies three times a year: Thanksgiving, Christmas, and the Fourth of July. When the word got out that he'd finished a batch, a bunch of Dad's relatives and friends would come by the house, asking for one. He made ten or fifteen of them at a crack, happily commandeering our kitchen for the better part of a weekend.

One year, when I was fifteen or sixteen—I can't remember what month it was, but I know it was a Saturday morning—the aroma of apple pie began wafting into my bedroom. I went downstairs and asked, "Hey, Dad, what'cha up to?"

He said, "I'm making some pies."

"But you only make pies three times a year. Fourth of July, Christmas, and Thanksgiving. What's this about?"

"I'm trying out a new recipe."

"A *new* recipe! Why are you trying a new recipe? You make the best apple pies in the world! You can't get better than best."

Dad smiled as if he knew some kind of secret—which he did.

"Oh yes, you can," he said. "I want to see if I can make 'best' even better."

Obviously, this did not feel like "work" to him. Now someone else walking into the kitchen and seeing all the utensils, measuring devices, flour all over the place, butter, sugar, cinnamon, and nutmeg laid out, with apples everywhere, waiting to be peeled and sliced, might have called it work. But to my father, it was pure joy—*literally*, the apple of his eye.

I learned that day from my Dad that just because doing something requires much work, that does not mean it has to be arduous or onerous. And as my Dad understood regarding his pies, it's not about getting things right.

He'd already gotten that right. But the human definition of "best" expands as we find joy in doing something well. That's only natural.

Wait. There's a better word. It's not just *natural*, it's actually *organic*. It's built *into us* at a cellular level. The more we do, the more we want to do. The farther we go, the farther we want to go. The higher we fly, the higher we want to fly. The more we understand, the more we want to understand.

And the more awakened we are, the more awakened we want to be.

THE INVITATIONS CONTINUE

This is the process by which we evolve. Indeed, I was told in my dialogue with God that the whole *purpose* of life is to *recreate ourselves anew,* continually reaching for the next grandest version of the greatest vision ever we held about who we are.

I was still surprised to learn, many years after publication of the first *Conversations with God* book—and following two decades of sharing its messages around the world—that I wasn't finished with this work.

I had never stopped having brief, private exchanges with the Divine about personal matters during those years, even when I thought that my *book-length* discussions for public consumption were a thing of the past.

So, the urgent feeling that overtook me in the pre-dawn hours of August 2, 2016 did more than awaken me from a sound sleep. It awakened me out of what I now describe as a temporary "consciousness lull," during which I could not see that there was more to be done. My invitation to continue to work with others in the world had not been withdrawn.

Nor, may I now say, has the invitation been withdrawn from you.

You, too, might feel that you've met your share of life challenges, solved your share of problems, and moved through your share of struggles. You might think you've done your share in many positive ways to offer support to others. But that does not mean your invitations have come to an end.

So, if you wake up some morning in the future to find yourself facing yet another such moment, see it as an opportunity to have a talk with God to determine how you can work this latest turn in your road into your life's continuing journey, without taking you off course.

You're up for it, I promise. You *came* here to experience self-creation at the highest level, and you've done wonderfully so far. You're ready for that next challenge.

We're all doing the same work, each in our own way. And that work is meant to be a *joy*, not a *job*. In the truest sense of the words, *a labor of love* awaits, opening you to a full experience of yourself even more extraordinary than all the times in the past when you've offered wonderful expressions of who you are.

Expect the challenges to come. Allow yourself to feel grateful for them. The movement into that energy—counterintuitive though it may seem— might be just the shift you need. It might be all that it takes to empower you to create the next grandest version of the greatest vision ever you held about who you are.

There are some tips and some tools that might be helpful in that regard. They're next, in Part Three. See what you think.

Neale Donald Walsch

PART THREE

Putting it All Together

There are more things in Heaven and Earth, Horatio,
than are dreamt of in your philosophy.

—WILLIAM SHAKESPEARE

TOOLS TO OPEN YOUR COMMUNICATION WITH GOD

———o O o———

O kay, let's bring together everything we've said on these extraordinary ideas, so they can be *used* and have a wonderfully beneficial *effect* on your life.

Having talks with God is not as difficult as the idea might at first seem, but it is best to begin with a clear understanding of exactly what is meant and what is not meant by the term.

As I noted in Part One of this book, some people feel that *praying* is having a conversation with the Divine. Often, however, praying is not a two-way encounter. Most people I've spoken to say they experience prayer as the fervent sending of a message to a higher power. This could be a supplication or a word of thanks, but it rarely constitutes a "conversation" as we understand the word. It's more of a monologue.

The dictionary defines *conversation* as "a talk, especially an informal one, between two or more people, in which news and ideas are exchanged." This is exactly the experience I first had with God beginning in the Spring of 1992, and of which I kept a written record for years after that. Many of the ideas that were exchanged stopped me in my tracks, as they contradicted what I'd been taught or had heard about life.

This might happen to you as well—not just the conversation, but the contradictions. So prepare to be surprised. Don't expect your interactions with the Divine to always confirm or duplicate what you think you already know, or what you have come to firmly believe. It could turn out that way in some cases—but in other cases, you might be invited to reflect on something that you have never considered or imagined.

That said, please let me remind you: Communications from the Divine never encourage or invite negative actions that could hurt, injure, or damage others.

I have been asked many times how people can have their own conversations with God, and so I studied my own experience carefully. I've come up with an informal process that I hope will help others.

ACCEPT THE POSSIBILITY

The first step is to hold as a possibility the existence of a God at all. So, I call Step One: Possibility. You can't talk to someone who is not there. You can't converse with someone who you do not even think exists, and many people—I mean, *millions*—do not believe in a higher power. Somewhere near 15 percent of the human race rejects the notion of a supreme being.

Now I'm guessing that you're not one of them, or you wouldn't be reading this book. But I've learned not to assume anything. You might be an atheist who wonders whether you're right about that and came here out of idle curiosity as to what others were claiming to be their experience. Or you could be a person who has been "on the fence" for years and you are looking for a nudge one way or the other.

So I'm going to risk sounding a bit simplistic here and repeat that Step One is the holding of a firm—and I do mean a *firm*—belief in the Divine.

Once you agree with yourself that there *is* such a thing as God, then you can move to a second possibility—one that's often a little more difficult for even believers in God to accept. You must believe that human beings can actually have two-way communications with this Divine essence.

This extends to accepting that such two-way exchanges are not only *possible*, but that they are occurring right now, and have *always* occurred, in the experience of humanity.

EMBRACE YOUR WORTHINESS

The second step in having your own talk with God is to include yourself in the circle of those you consider to be *worthy* of such experiences. So I call Step Two: Worthiness.

Many folks already believe that humans have had conversations with God. Moses said he did, and many accepted him at his word. The messages he received have formed the basis of an entire religion. Jesus said he was speaking for God directly, and many have accepted him at his word. The messages he received also have formed the basis of an entire religion. Muhammad, bless his holy name, said he was inspired by God directly, and many accepted him at his word. The messages he received also have formed the basis of an entire religion.

Hildegard of Bingen has been recognized since the Middle Ages as a mystic and visionary who wrote the world's oldest surviving morality play, *Ordo Virtutum.* Joseph Smith said an angel led him to plates on which were engraved messages directly from God. Those messages have also formed the basis of an entire religion.

Bahá'u'lláh felt that he was Divinely inspired, and many believed him. The messages he received have formed the basis of yet another entire religion. Teresa of Ávila was canonized as a saint by the Catholic Church after having experienced, and written about, a way for ordinary people to move into mystical union with God.

So millions have already acknowledged that *some* human beings have had precisely these kinds of experiences. Why, then, couldn't we?

Perhaps it is because we think that those other human beings are somehow more special than we are. They're more holy or they're more wise. Or we think they're more pure or more *something*. They are something that we are not.

Yet the fact is, they are *nothing* we are not. So the second step of the process leading to your own conversation with God is to acknowledge your worthiness—that you are just as worthy as anyone else to be spoken to by God.

BE READY, WILLING, AND ABLE

The third step in the process is to move to a place of willingness to receive such communications—and that must manifest itself in behaviors that *demonstrate* willingness. I call Step Three: Willingness.

For instance, I set aside a few minutes each day for quiet contemplation. I don't keep running my life as if I don't have time for contemplation. I demonstrate a willingness to receive such communications from God by preserving and arranging for sufficient time for that to occur, and by creating conditions in my environment that allow it to occur. I arise in the morning and I try very hard to spend some quiet time thinking and writing before I do anything else.

On some days I might also do some in-place meditating. We don't have to go to a special room, sit down and light a candle, or put on some special music to meditate. That's a nice thing to do, but it's not required. We can meditate anywhere. Right where you are when you decide to meditate, you can do just that. Lying in bed just after you awaken. Sitting in the kitchen while the coffee is brewing. Standing under a rainbow after a summer shower.

And meditation does not have to look a certain way. It can look like gentle observation or thinking—but thinking from the level of *soul*, not the level of mind. This is really not thinking at all, but a "bringing through" of wisdom from *another level* of life. I call that level "God."

Whatever it looks like to you, work some quiet time into your daily routine, and you'll be surprised at how easy it is to commune with the Divine.

With me, it's not the same every day, but I do give myself time every morning to be alone with my soul. If I miss that time in the morning—if life just will not allow me to have that time on a certain day—then I make sure that I find *some* time during that day to just stop and give myself even ten seconds of peace.

This is what I call "stopping meditation."

It's when you just stop everything you're doing, for ten blessed seconds, and do nothing … say nothing… *think* nothing. Just *be*.

You can make this happen at any time. You can stop while walking down the street, while doing the dishes, or sometimes right in the middle of writing a sen….

What I described just now is unusual, I'm sad to say. Most people live their whole lives and give their mind a rest once or twice a month. They get inspired, read a book, and think *I'll try it!*—but after three days, they stop and get back to "regular life."

Yet if this becomes a regular part of regular life—if you set aside a time to commune with your soul every day—after a few days, you'll find that you're having the "conversations with God" you've heard me talk about.

God communes with us in the spaces *between* our thoughts, not during our thoughts. Or better yet, I should say that God talks *all* the time, but we can *hear* God better in the spaces between our thoughts—and between our actions, too. Because at those times, our thoughts and actions are not getting in the way.

Just be *willing* to hear God, and demonstrate this by giving yourself some holy moments each day to just listen.

STAY WIDE AWAKE

The fourth step is a commitment to wakefulness; an agreement you make with yourself to *pay attention to God*. So I call Step Four: Wakefulness.

God is all around us, and many of us are not paying attention. We may be *willing*… we might have gone past Step Three… but we're not *awake*, and we're not paying attention.

Sometimes, ironically, we pay *too much* attention. We're *looking too hard* for what's right in front of our faces. We're listening so earnestly that we miss the sound.

God is talking to us in a thousand different ways, across a million moments. But we must cultivate what I call "attentive *inattention*"…or unexpected expectation, or active inactivity.

This is when you listen by not listening. It is when you look by not looking. It is when you open your mind's ear and your mind's eye to nothing at all, expecting nothing at all. In that moment, you are searching for nothing at all, wishing for nothing at all, striving for nothing at all… you are just being with "no thing/everything."

This *attentive inattention* turns *every* moment into a meditation. Just let life go by, but watch it out of the corner of your eye, the corner of your *third* eye!

God's conversations will sneak up on you. He might deliver his message through the lyrics of the next song you hear on the overhead speakers in the department store or the article that jumps off the cover of a two-year-old magazine at the hair salon. His words might be in a chance utterance of a friend you just happen to meet on the street or on the billboard around the next corner... or they might be a fleeting thought that crosses your mind, seemingly out of nowhere.

Nowhere... that's an interesting word. Slice it in half and it comes out to Now Here. God is always *Now Here.*

Don't sleepwalk through life. Stay awake. Watch what's going on—but without looking for something in particular.

Like right now. *What do you think is happening right now?*

CALL IT WHAT IT IS

Step Five is Acceptance ...or, if you please, non-denial. We need to call our talks with God exactly what they are when they occur.

Once we start setting aside that special time for God, and then begin walking through life in wakefulness, we will be aware that we are receiving communications from the Divine all the time. Now, suddenly, we will *notice* them. We will become aware that life informs us *about* life through the process of living. And we will become a conscious part of that process.

Still, if we're not careful, we'll be tempted—as I mentioned in earlier writing here—to call this something else. We'll give it a label or a name that people can accept. We'll call it anything and everything *except* a conversation with God. And in denying it for what it is, we will minimize it. That's the danger. We won't give God's message the importance it deserves, because we're calling it less than it is.

Now there's another side to this. And it's kind of ironic, but I have to tell you about it, so you don't fall into the trap.

CURB YOUR ENTHUSIASM

You will want to be careful not to become *so* emotionally attached to the possibility of this experience that you start categorizing *everything that happens* as "a sign" or "God, talking to me." Step Six is Discernment.

In other words, don't let your imagination run away with you. Don't let your mind play tricks on you.

God talks to you through your soul, not through your mind. And yes, *you can learn to tell the difference.* This is called *discernment*.

If you're reaching for your car keys and a dollar falls out of your pocket onto the sidewalk, this might not be "a sign" that you should take all the money out of your pocket and throw it on the ground.

If you turn on your laptop in the morning and it's taking forever to load its programs, and then begins to malfunction, this may not necessarily be "a sign" that you should throw out your computer.

Be judicious. Give everything the "tummy test." Your stomach will know when something is true. Ever notice that? The tummy knows what the mind can only wonder about.

The body is more intelligent than we think. Listen to your body. Notice how you feel. If you feel *uplifted* by something you have noticed out of the "corner of your eye," pay attention to that. If you feel downtrodden or burdened by an incoming communication, it cannot be directly from God. It must be from your mind. Or… it has been filtered so much *by* your mind that you have lost the purity of the original communication.

THE MIND'S IMPORTANT JOB

Now don't get me wrong. Your mind is not your enemy. It is a very important and effective tool and it has a job to do: to ensure your survival. Therefore, your mind will always look for anything that might seem to threaten you. It will be super-cautious. It will see every possible bad outcome and warn you about it. That's why you will often feel burdened instead of uplifted by its communications.

And then, irony of ironies, when your mind sees that you are feeling burdened, it will do whatever it can to guarantee that you get through that "downer" so that you can survive. It might even give you a temporary "high"—such as a thought that every single thing that you experience is a "sign from God." If *that* doesn't make you feel special, nothing will.

So be careful with your mind. It is always powerful, but not always reliable. Use discernment. Go to the place that's *thinking about what you're thinking about.* This is *who you really are.* You are the observer of that which is being observed.

You are neither your body nor your mind nor your soul—you are all three, combined.

This is the totality of your being—and this is what you are seeking to experience during your time here on Earth. If you feel you have had a moment of closeness with, and communication from, God, hold it in a special way. Whether it was a suddenly appearing shooting star, an inexplicable impulse to slam on your car's brakes, or an actual, two-way exchange that filled your heart, let that moment serve you at the highest level. Accept it as evidence of a truth that your soul has been working to place before you from the very beginning: that during your time here on Earth, you are never alone.

In short, you really *are* having *conversations with God* all the time. And it's my hope that, with the use of the six steps I've laid out here, you can experience those conversations empowered, deliberately, and with intention.

STRIKE WHILE THE IRON IS HOT

$\Longrightarrow\!\circ\,O\,\circ\!\Longleftarrow$

xperiencing a direct communication from the Divine can have a profound effect on any individual. What is the most beneficial way to respond, if and when we feel that we've had such an experience?

First, it's important to know is that there is no requirement around this. There is nothing that God needs you to do, expects you to do, or demands that you do. So gently step away from any worry about how God might react to how you react.

The second thing is, it's important to know is that it is not unusual to be stunned by your experience. The energetic encounter—especially the first one, if you eventually have a two-way conversation—may well produce emotions of awe, wonder, and even disbelief.

I chose not to shrug off the message I'd been given, and I'm going to offer this advice to you: After you have used your discernment to decide which thoughts, concepts, and ideas really are coming directly from God, give yourself permission to act on them. Do something about them *now*, instead of putting them on a mental pile for *later*.

STEP INTO ACTION

When I was a child, there used to be a saying: "Strike while the iron is hot."

To forge something from steel, you must pound the metal into the desired form while it is white hot, when it is pliable enough to turn into anything you want.

When you have a conversation with God, something wants to be forged from solid matter. So strike while the iron is hot. *Do it. Act on it. Step into it*, not away from it.

And do it now, not tomorrow. Not when you have more time, more money, or *whatever it is* you think you don't have enough of right now.

Make it your intention to at least begin. Perhaps it is true that you don't have a particular item, or a particular aspect, perfectly in place. But make it your intention to *begin*. And then... make it your intention to *complete*.

Remember that *life proceeds out of your intentions for it*. Completion is one indication of enlightenment. Notice how much lighter you feel when you complete *anything*.

In the book titled *The Only Thing That Matters*, I offered the observation that 98 percent of the world's people are spending 98 percent of their time on things that don't matter. Your life, it says, has to do with how you seek to reach *completion* on the journey of the soul.

Can this be true? Can it be that our time on Earth was never intended to be focused mainly on our physical experience, but on our *metaphysical* experience?

It can be true, and it is.

And...here's the best part: Going where your soul seeks to go, experiencing what your soul seeks to experience, and expressing what your soul seeks to express, does not mean denying yourself "the good life." In fact, letting your soul guide you will go far toward *ensuring* you find the good life.

Completion of the soul's agenda does not require that you forego, shun, or renounce what your body and your mind enjoy. It is not about giving up one aspect of life for another, in a sort of unending version of Lent.

If you pay attention to your soul's agenda and to what it invites you to do, the rest of life will take care of itself. It will take *care* of itself *by* itself. Or, to paraphrase a far more eloquent statement: Don't go around asking, "*What are we to eat? What are we to drink? Wherewithal shall we clothe ourselves?" Seek ye first the Kingdom of Heaven, and all these things will be added unto you.*

The "Kingdom of Heaven" and "completion of the sacred journey" refer to the same thing. When you experience the second, you experience the first. The problem with both phrases is that no one has lately (if ever) explained how to seek the Kingdom of Heaven.

The Kingdom of Heaven is, of course, not merely a physical location. It is the state of being *complete*. Done. Finished. Over with the search for self. Through with looking for peace, answers, and reasons. And so, it is perfect that the two phrases are used here interchangeably.

It is literally "heaven" for humans to find themselves in a state in which they are clear that there is nothing left they need to be, do, or have, to experience inner peace, unconditional love, and the gentle bliss of sweet (as opposed to angry, aloof, or "holier-than-thou") detachment. All the inner peace that is, and all that one could ever desire, is fully present and can be experienced *right here, right now*. One merely needs to stop resisting what the current moment is presenting and remember that "What you resist, persists, and what you look at ceases to have its illusory form."

Once we see the illusion as what it is and realize that nothing and no one can touch us in any way that can hurt, injure, anger, frustrate, disappoint, or damage our souls—we are *complete*.

The soul's agenda is to bring you to this very state, so that you may recreate yourself anew in each *golden moment of now* and become the next grandest version of the greatest vision ever you held about *who you are*. In this way, you can overcome exterior events or circumstances impacting the body or the mind.

Borrowing again from *The Only Thing That Matters*, being *complete* creates the space for that aspect of life that is called "you" to express, experience, reflect, demonstrate, and personify that aspect of life that is called Divinity.

So, intend to *begin*—and intend to *complete*—the next step in the process of your own evolution. Don't wonder about what it is you should do in the next moment of your life. Don't worry about what, in specific terms, your next step should be, or the exact way to deal with your current dilemma. Instead, say this prayer:

> *Thank you, God, for helping me*
> *to understand that this problem*
> *has already been solved for me.*

Ask God whatever you wish to ask. Then listen, watch, and wait. Listen for the answer.

TRY IT RIGHT NOW

Let's have some joy and engage this process right now. I'm going to invite you to formulate any question that you would like to ask God in this moment.

Take out a piece of paper and a pen and write that question down. Make it a question that's important to you—not something frivolous, like who's going to win the Kentucky Derby or what's the lucky lottery number. Write down something that matters to your heart and your soul.

Go ahead. Take a moment right now and write that down.

Good.

Now I want you to know that this question *will* be answered. It will be answered instantly. Indeed, it has been written: "Even before you ask, I will have answered."

Yet you might not hear the answer in this very moment. You may not be aware of it "right now." This is important to understand before you engage the *Conversations with God* process.

There is no right or wrong way to experience this. If you do not instantly know the answer that God is giving you, do not make yourself or the process "wrong." Go into it without expectation. Not everyone becomes aware of their conversation with God in the same way.

Let that be okay. Otherwise, you'll run the risk of wanting too much for it to happen or *needing* too much for it to occur right now, in one particular way. Keep in mind the very act of wanting a thing pushes it away from you. This is because your urgent expression of *wanting* says to the universe that *you do not now have it*. And this is the reality you will experience because whatever you declare with energy and consistency will receive only one answer from God: Yes.

Remember that.

God only says "yes."

So if you declare, "I want more *money* in my life!" God will say, "Yes, that's true. You do." And if you say, "Doggone it, I want my perfect *partner*," God will say, "Yes, that's true. You do." And then you'll wonder, "What's wrong with me that I never get what I want?" because you don't understand the laws of metaphysics. You don't understand that as you speak it, so will it be done unto you—especially if you speak it with vehemence, with power, with high energy, and with consistency.

So stay out of this trap. Give yourself time. Have patience with yourself and with the process. When you deliberately ask a question of God, you ultimately will become aware of the answer. This will likely happen sooner if you stop fearfully looking for it or demanding it with frustration and just let it "come to you."

Ask, and you will be answered. Knock, and it will be opened unto you. So let yourself receive the answer in the fullness of time. Let it all be okay.

NOW LET'S TALK *ABOUT* GOD

W e've taken a deep dive here into ways of having conversations *with* God, but I don't want to leave this whole exploration of the higher power without engaging in more conversations *about* God—and inviting you to do so also, with people you know.

Remember how I said that Step One in having your own talk with God is agreeing to the possibility that God even exists, and how I then observed that millions across the world don't think so? I believe it would serve all of us to speak more often and more openly about this topic.

Most people don't like to talk about God because they're afraid that talking about God will lead to disagreements. And, in truth, it *might*, as people hold a wide variety of thoughts on this subject. So, one of the many messages we've been given in our society about how to get along with others is to never talk about religion or politics in polite company.

I bring up this message for a reason. We are best advised to look at it carefully, to see if it serves us. We will benefit from considering that it comes to us via a species-wide, culturally generated *message delivery system* that is very much a part of our daily experience.

Messages come at us from every angle: some as a direct instruction, some as an off-handed comment, some from life's authority figures, and some from people we've never met or heard of.

You might find it a bit amusing to look at some of what we've been told as I illustrate this point.

MESSAGES OF MADNESS

We've been told about the "survival of the fittest," that "to the victor go the spoils," that "nice guys finish last," and that "the one with the most toys wins."

We've been told that "it's every man for himself" and "the end justifies the means." We've learned that "money doesn't grow on trees" and that "you're to be seen and not heard."

We've been told to "never color outside the lines" and that "you made your bed and now you have to lie in it." We've been told that "it's us against them," that "you can't fight City Hall," that "you can't have your cake and eat it, too," and to "never count your chickens before they hatch."

We've been told "don't cast your pearls before swine," "don't change horses in midstream," "don't cut off your nose to spite your face," "don't put the cart before the horse," "don't throw good money after bad," "don't throw the baby out with the bath water," and, *above all*, "don't upset the apple cart."

I call these our society's Messages of Madness. Some of them are even *totally contradictory.*

Birds of a feather flock together / Opposites attract.

Nothing ventured, nothing gained / Better safe than sorry.

Curiosity killed the cat / What you don't know can't hurt you.

He who hesitates is lost / Look before you leap.

Many hands make light work / Too many cooks spoil the broth.

There's no such thing as a free lunch / The best things in life are free.

Yikes!

Then—and here's where it is not at all amusing, and very much more critical—there are the things you've been told about God.

We've been told that we need to obey God's commands, do God's will, follow God's law, and fear God's wrath. We've been told that when we face God's judgment, we will be begging for God's mercy—and, depending on our offenses, we may not get it, but could face being condemned to everlasting and unbearable torture in the fires of hell.

The point of all the above: Our minds have been filled with many, many messages that have created the foundation for a day-to-day reality so far removed from our real reason for being on the Earth that it's a wonder we can experience any joy or excitement on the journey at all... much less clarity regarding what the whole thing is about.

Now along comes a new message: Ignore the injunction against talking about God in polite company. Bring the subject *up*.

IS THERE MORE TO KNOW?

I have an idea that one reason the topic of God has brought us to such a place of challenge, and even violence, in our global society through the years is that our understanding of God might be incomplete. I have this thought that maybe, just *maybe*, there is something still left to uncover here, something still left to know, and that uncovering and knowing it could change everything.

What do you think? Does this seem possible? Could there be something that most people don't know about God, the knowing of which would profoundly alter, in a very positive way, our experience of life on Earth?

We keep uncovering new information in the field of, say, science all the time. Scientists understand that the moment they think they know everything about something, they close off every possibility for a brighter tomorrow, because the assumption that we know everything science has to show us means that we can't go any further than where we are right now.

Humanity has reached its peak in this field of endeavor. But, of course, that is not true, and scientists know it.

We keep uncovering new information in the field of, say, medicine. Medical researchers understand that the moment they think they know everything about something, they close off every possibility for a brighter tomorrow, because the assumption that we know everything medicine has to show us means that we can't go any further than where we are right now. Humanity has reached its peak in this field of endeavor. But, of course, that is not true, and medical researchers know it.

We keep uncovering new information in the field of, say, technology. People in technology understand that the moment they think they know everything about something, they close off every possibility for a brighter tomorrow, because the assumption that we know everything technology has to show us means that we can't go any further than where we are right now. Humanity has reached its peak in this field of endeavor. But, of course, that is not true, and those working in technology know it.

Forgive the repetition, but there's a point to be made here.

Could it possibly be that *theology* might also have something new to uncover? If the answer is no, then all possibility for a brighter tomorrow ends because the assumption that we know everything theology has to show us means that we can't go any further than where we are right now. It means humanity has reached its peak in this field of endeavor.

Now, is it any more true in the area of theology than it is in science, medicine, or technology that we have discovered it all? Have we reached the height of our theological awareness? Is there not even a tiny bit of data about God that we do not now have? And if there *is* something we do not fully understand, how might we come to a greater understanding? By refusing to talk about it in polite company?

I don't think so.

My observation has shown me that even though many people don't wish to talk about it, they don't mind fighting about it. Can that possibly be the more polite thing to do?

Of course not.

So, let's not stop at having conversations *with* God. Let's have conversations *about* God. And let's be the ones to *begin* such conversations. Yes, in polite company.

Dare you, dare you, "double-dare" you.

SHARE A DIFFERENT STORY

Many of our religions and cultures teach us that God is "over there," and we are "over here," and that our job is to get back "over there." Our challenge, this ancient story tells us, is to return to God. We must move through the life that we are living now—our time of travail—in a particular way if we hope to make that return trip.

I am simplifying things here, but this is the way that millions of people think of life's purpose. You might wish to offer a different thought, propose a different idea, or share a different story.

How about the story that was articulated earlier, in Part One, in the chapter Is God Listening? To save you from having to look it up: We are *not* separated from God, and we never have been. Such a thing is impossible, for there is *nothing that God is not.* Invite others to try that one on for size.

There is only *one thing*, expressing itself in countless ways. This single, Divine essence is the energy of life itself—and thus, it is *who you are.* There is no separation between yourself and the Divine because, by definition, there cannot be.

Only if God is *not* the higher power—only if God is *not* the essential essence that is everywhere present—can separation of any kind exist.

If separation does exist, then we really *are* "children of a lesser god" (which was the title of a smash 1980 Broadway play, and a hit 1986 movie, with the phrase taken from the eleventh chapter of Alfred Lord Tennyson's *Idylls of the King*: "For why is all around us here, as if some lesser god had made the world.")

Yet we are no such thing, and when we understand this, we begin to *embody* it. We experience that God is not something *outside of us* that we need to beg for help, but rather, something *inside* of us that we may call on. We can call it *forth* because it exists *in* us, *as* us.

Now, if you are wondering how you can bring yourself insights on the way to proceed in a situation where you don't have a notion as to what those insights might be, the answer is this: You can cultivate your ability to hear that "still, small voice *within*." In other words...(ahem)... decide to have *a talk... a conversation with God.*

If you do, you will find that God has never left you and never deserted you. God has merely been waiting for you to find your way to God. And *then* you will discover not only peace and relief from stress, but amazing solutions and answers to life's daily challenges and problems. Ideas and inspirations will come to you; if you trust these and act on them, you will emerge victorious over your troubles.

This, at least, has been my experience—which is why I will never stop engaging in *GodTalk*. I hope this book has helped you to start, or encouraged you to continue, your conversation with God and that you will never, ever stop.

LET'S ALSO TALK ABOUT WAKING UP

———————o O o———————

n Step Four, I described having your own conversation with God as *wakefulness*. Our challenge on Earth today is that the place is full of sleepwalkers. If the sleepwalkers were happy, I would say, let 'em sleep! But they're not. They're miserable. They are—if we can speak in metaphors— walking into walls and stepping off cliffs. They are bumping into each other, knocking each other down, and trampling all over each other.

They're crying out in pain, whimpering in their suffering, shouting out in anger, and swearing in frustration. They grumble and growl and grouse their way through the absolute nightmare they've created.

Worse yet, some people are now wondering if it's better to be asleep than awake. This insane thought ignores the very reason we brought ourselves here—that is, voluntarily placed our souls into a physical body in the first place. But in this nightmare-made-into-reality, insanity is sometimes preferred over sanity, irrationality over rationality, and fear over love.

The definition of *insanity* is doing the same thing over and over again, expecting to get a different result. That's what we're doing, all over this planet. That is what sleepwalkers do. They prefer doing the same thing again and again because doing something new might just wake them out of their slumber.

Conversations with God told us that humanity is a relatively young species in the universe. This must be true because the people of our world act like little children. We're insulting, threatening, and battling with each other. We're killing each other when we disagree.

I feel sure that if sentient beings living on other planets saw this happening there, they'd simply stop it. But not here on Earth. Here, we just keep repeating the same behaviors, expecting to get different results.

It's a nightmare created by sleepwalkers going around in circles, and the only answer is to wake people up. But the question is: *How can we wake people up?*

I think if we really do decide to talk about God—even as we talk with God—we will benefit greatly, because the invitation before us today from life itself involves nothing less than the awakening of humanity.

Can humanity be awakened? Is our species *capable* of waking up, or are we destined to die in our sleep?

Surely, we can see now that Al Gore was right about what he called "the inconvenient truth" of global warming. Surely, we can see now that Gloria Steinem was right about the need to recognize, and to end, the diminution, subjugation, and oppression of women. Surely, we can see now that Martin Luther King Jr. was right about the need for the civil rights movement to move forward immediately and in earnest.

Can we also see that we are right to assert that humanity needs to bring an end to *separation theology*, and to create a *new spirituality* on Earth?

Of course, we understand that in the literal sense of the words, "right" and "wrong" do not exist. We have been talking here about "what works" and "what does not work," given what it is we, as a species, are trying to do.

And what is our goal? We are trying to survive as long as we can. And why? Simply to get to a ripe old age? No, I believe it's about more than that.

In my understanding, we are here on Earth, in physical bodies, to serve a larger purpose. I believe we are here to move forward with the *agenda of the soul,* which is focused on turning our *knowledge* of who we are into our *experience* of who we are.

This idea is not universally embraced in human society today. But people who are clear that this is our goal are keenly aware that being in the realm of the physical is the central ingredient in serving the soul's agenda. This is the only realm with the right conditions to make it possible.

So yes, we are trying to survive as long as we can in our physical form, in order to move forward in completing our agenda. But the largest percentage of humans do not yet understand that we will require a totally revised definition of God and a vastly expanded awareness of the purpose of life if we wish to guarantee *joy-filled* survival, and not misery-laden survival, for ourselves, our children, and our grandchildren.

That is why conversations *about* God are vitally important right now. So let me emphasize that we would benefit enormously from talking about God openly, freely, and frequently, and from deeply exploring with each other the purpose of life. We might broach the subject at our dinner tables, during casual get-togethers of family and friends, in lunchroom chats with coworkers, while conversing with our grown children in Facetime or Zoom visits, and yes, even—and perhaps especially—as part of social gatherings with fellow members of our temple, synagogue, or church.

Conversations with God says that "life informs life about life through the process of life itself." The kinds of dialogues I've suggested above are just some of the ways that life can do this.

THE BIGGEST IDEA YOU COULD EVER SHARE

———○○○———

*T*he future can be brighter today, and the world can be better today, because you are on the Earth right now. Do you know that? *It's true.* Each piece of loving and healing energy that you bring to the moments of your life is also brought to the moments of the lives of others, because even *thinking* of another in a loving and healing way sends those energies to them. In this way, just being the loving, caring, and giving person that you are changes the world that you touch.

You have enormous power within you. God works through you, *as you.* To the extent that you allow this to occur consciously, as an *intentioned event,* you become a messenger. So many have been waiting for your message.

I have not chosen those words lightly. Each of us can be a messenger, but only a few of us know it. We can remind each other of *who we really are.* If enough of us do it, we can change so much on this planet.

That is what all of humanity's wonderful spiritual teachers—female and male, in ancient times and in contemporary times—set out to do. The only difference between us and those who have been recognized as wonderful spiritual teachers is that they remembered who they really were, and we have forgotten—unless we have not.

In the moment of our remembering, we join those teachers in consciousness. We become *one* in consciousness with the only consciousness there is. Once we have discovered this secret, many of us float in and out of that one consciousness during the days of our lives. The great spiritual teachers simply remained there. We can remain there, too—or we can, at least, reside there a lot longer than most of us do now.

Do you know how to do that? There is a trick to it, and it's easy.

The way to remain in a higher state of consciousness, connected to the *one consciousness that is*, is to help *another* person remain there. That is why I am inviting you to talk more often and more openly about God. It is why each of the great teachers did what *they* did, spending their lives reminding everyone else that we are all one with God, and one with each other.

The great spiritual teachers did this by sharing a big, very specific idea. I am going to invite you to explore, and then to share, this huge idea as well. You've very likely considered it in your life before—perhaps not as comprehensively as it will be explored here, but you have probably entertained it prior to this reading.

The idea itself is not new. The revolutionary part is that you may be embracing it, then deciding to implement it "full out," and even to openly share it with others for the first time.

This is the biggest idea you could ever share. It's an idea that can utterly and completely change the way you, and those you share it with, live your life. It can change the *reason* you live your life, everything you say you want *out* of your life, and everything you are going to put *into* it.

THE BIG IDEA

Here, then, is the grandest notion ever held in the mind of humans. It is also the oldest impulse ever felt, and the deepest desire ever held by any sentient being: We *are*, in fact—just as we have been told by many religions—made in the image and likeness of God.

Let me repeat that, so its importance doesn't escape either of us.

We are made in the image and likeness of God.

Do everything in your power right now to resist any temptation to respond to that with, "Yes, yes, I've heard this all before." Having *heard it* before has meant nothing to most people. Until I was well past sixty years old, those were just words to me.

Now, however, we're all being invited to put those words into action and to let them mean something—not just broadly speaking, as a concept, but in a specific way, as the *daily basis* for every choice, decision, and action.

This big idea is not religious dogma, wishful thinking, or spiritual metaphor. *Science* has placed it in a new category. Science is now telling us that we are each made of the stuff of which *everything* is made. We are each individuated manifestations of the primal force, the undifferentiated energy, the essential essence from which all of life emerges and which all of life expresses.

We are each Divine. Life is now inviting us to demonstrate Divinity. We are each aspects of God, and life is asking us to make that understanding practical and *functional* in our daily experience.

Is such a thing realistic? Is such a thing possible? Let's see if we can find a theoretical basis in physical reality for this very big assumption.

Remember when I spoke earlier about medicine, and what it has newly uncovered? Well, I'm sure you know that medical science uncovered relatively recently—in the early 1960s, to be exact—that the human body contains stem cells, undifferentiated cells that can be coaxed into becoming any cell of the body that is needed, and then persuaded to reproduce.

Now if medical science of that young species in the cosmos called "humans" can produce such an outcome, using their just-recently-acquired knowledge, what do you imagine the *source of the universe*—however you conceive of it—can do?

Would it be terribly inaccurate to call the undifferentiated energy, life's essential essence, the "stem cells" of the universe? I don't think so. But I have given this primal force another name: I have called it God. I have described it as Divine.

THE IDEA BEHIND THE IDEA

The hypothesis here is that when you express the undifferentiated essence of the universe, you project an *energy* that is *generic*. It is constant and singular, unwavering and unchanging, precisely because it *is* "undifferentiated."

At the highest level, this pure energy is conscious and aware of itself, because it is *consciousness* and *awareness* itself. It is that from which all differentiated consciousness and awareness springs. This primal force and prime source wants and needs nothing, for the simple and elegant reason that it *is* everything it could possibly want.

More and more human beings are now understanding this. More and more of us are beginning to comprehend that all of us are emanations of the *same single thing*. We are the product of it and the possessors of it. We can also be the projectors of it.

As such, we are in charge of more than we might imagine—including our future. Life is simply waiting for us to *take* charge.

Every spiritual master has told us that we can do this by demonstrating Divinity. Every spiritual teacher has told us that, in this way, we are making God practical and making God real—in us, as us, and through us.

WHAT'S STOPPING US FROM LIVING THIS TRUTH

What we've been discussing here—living and demonstrating that we are each made in the image and likeness of God—might at first appear to be a naïvely idealistic and utterly impractical approach to meeting global challenges and solving life's problems. Yet it is a readily available and immediately accessible formula for transforming our individual experience and healing our planet. And it is more easily applicable than any solution that most human beings have ever seriously considered.

That's *why* it at first seems impractical: *Few people have ever tried it.*

How many is "few"? Mere hundreds across the entire span of human history. That's *hundreds* out of hundreds of *billions* who have lived on the earth. And this is the reason that the global experience of humanity has not been more elevated. We have perceived these few individuals whose experiences *have* been elevated as somehow different. We have called them saint, sage—and yes, savior.

Ironically, those elevated souls have *not* been different from us—*and this has been their most oft-repeated message*. They have told us, again and again, that demonstrating Divinity is within the reach of all human beings.

Why, then, do not more human beings reach for it?

Simple. They do not know how.

And here is a second irony. *Attempts to describe the process* have *kept* Divinity from being demonstrated. Telling others how to live as expressions of the Divine has caused so much anger, violence, and fear on this planet.

We have been told it is possible to share this information, but the directions have included following *this* teacher, accepting *this* savior, honoring *this* messenger, following *this* doctrine, or acting in *this* way—and then we find ourselves disagreeing. Then, as I have repeatedly observed, we battle each other and kill each other over our disagreements.

We've done it for centuries—actually, for millennia.

And lately, things have gone from bad to worse. We are driving around now with bumper stickers that say, "God, save me from Your people."

But—at last, and at least—we also are asking some piercing questions.

Is there any hope? Are we really nothing more than a species of sentient beings run amok, blowing up bombs under the ground to prove our invincibility? Ending people's lives by firing squad, or in electric chairs, or with a lethal injection, to demonstrate our righteousness? Allowing 653 children (by latest count) to die of starvation on our planet *every hour* as we defend a global economy that benefits, at the highest level, the smallest number of humans?

Have we so lost our collective mind that we think that the way to stop gun violence is for everybody in the world to carry a gun?

Have we so lost our collective will as to find no way to change the conditions that create refugee crises rendering thousands homeless and begging other countries for asylum?

Have we so lost our collective morals that we consider divisiveness, rudeness, insults, and tasteless verbal bullying to be the hallmark of leadership?

Is this what we have come to? Gun-toting, fist-pumping, verbal-bashing, jaw-jutting, loud-mouthed intimidators and strong-armed tyrants, daring anyone to stand up for what is gentle, peaceful, and—God forbid—loving?

If we can't even agree on how to disagree, can we at least agree on how to be agreeable? Can we become Divinely inspired, Divinely motivated, Divinely activated, Divinely expressed, and Divinely realized?

Yes.

Yes, we can.

But what the world needs now is a gentle, loving way to replace our fearful, righteous, and condemning approach to explaining how we may all both experience and express our highest selves—which is, in fact, our *true nature*—in everyday life.

We're being invited by life—and, in this moment, by this book!—to start conversations about God in polite company. We are being asked to end the illusion of separation and to embrace and *share* the truth that *we are all one—* and that each of us is made in the image and likeness of God.

And the wonder of this *one way to change everything* is that we can start in our own homes. This doesn't have to be a planetary political movement. It doesn't have to produce an immediate global and social transformation. It doesn't have to generate a worldwide spiritual renaissance. It can begin, as I suggested before, at our dinner tables, in our living rooms, by our kitchen sinks.

We can begin demonstrating Divinity in the immediate moment and in the immediate vicinity. We have been given the tools many times, by many messengers, and once again in the *Conversations with God* dialogues.

I chose to borrow passages above from the book titled *God's Message to the World: You've Got Me All Wrong*, because if we're going to fully understand the unconditionally loving and totally accepting deity described in *Conversations with God*, we'll want to deeply explore the logic behind the idea that God does not demand to be loved.

As you surely must know, many believe that the opposite is true. In what has been labeled as the greatest of the Ten Commandments, we read: "Thou shalt love the Lord thy God with all thy heart, and with all thy soul, and with all thy might." In other words, God *does* demand to be loved.

DO YOU AGREE?

Now I've been strongly suggesting that all of us talk more often and more openly about this God that we have heard about—but what shall we say? I mean, in short, what are we being invited to share?

I began articulating some of that in Part One of this book, and later I suggested we begin to share a different story about God. May I offer a few more words now, to clarify that? You might find the thoughts below helpful in arriving at just the articulation you need to make the points you wish to make. Unless, of course, you disagree with me. Let's see, shall we?

My suggestion: Let it be said, clearly and without equivocation, that the God of this universe—by *virtue* of *being* God—needs or requires the adulation of no one.

The God of this universe—by virtue of being God—has nothing to lose by welcoming any soul who arrives at Divinity by any path. God is nothing but overjoyed when any soul has found its way back home by realizing, accepting, and assuming its *true identity*.

The idea that God rejects everyone except those who come to God by a particular spiritual path or religion is simply mistaken. It defies all rational thought and directly contradicts the definition of pure love.

The good news is that our deity is not the God of the brand name. God's love, God's acceptance, and God's joy in us is not dependent upon what words we say in prayer, what name we invoke in supplication, or what faith we embrace in hopefulness. In the eyes of God, a Jew is as worthy of God's love as a Christian, a Christian is as worthy as a Muslim, a Muslim is as worthy as a Hindu, a Hindu is as worthy as a Buddhist, a Buddhist is as worthy as a Mormon, a Mormon is as worthy as a Bahá'í, and a Bahá'í is as worthy as a Taoist. An atheist is as worthy as all of the above.

Now I know this runs counter to the teachings of many religions, so the above statement is difficult for some people to believe. Yet *that which is* is *that which IS*, and neither its *Isness*, nor its joy and bliss in *being* the *Isness*, is dependent upon a particular expression, in any particular way, by any part of the Isness.

Let us go even further. It is not even necessary for human beings to have *any* belief that there *is* a God for God's blessings to flow. The flowing of God's blessings is God's greatest joy. The process is uninterrupted and eternal. It has nothing to do with *our* love for *God*, and everything to do with *God's* love for *us*.

This might be the toughest concept for human beings to accept. The largest number of humans just can't seem to embrace the notion that Divine love flows freely to all, without exception, requirement, or condition of any kind.

In a remarkable inversion, many humans declare that God's love *does* flow freely to all, and that God's judgment, condemnation, and punishment is a *demonstration* of God's love.

It is only through such convoluted theological architecture that they can preserve the idea of a "God kind and good"—although is it questionable if such preservation has been achieved at the level that those who have constructed this theology might have wished. There is far more evidence that the idea of a *God kind and good* has been forfeited by some of the world's largest religions. This might be the chief reason that 15 percent of the planet's population reject the idea of any sort of God at all.

This is one of the greatest sadnesses to have befallen humanity, for it has robbed so many members of the species of their greatest resource, therefore crippling the species immeasurably.

Hopefully, the God who is described by the many messengers of what has been called *the new spirituality* will be a deity that humans of the 21st century and beyond can embrace. What is needed on Earth now is a *civil rights movement for the soul*, freeing humanity at last from the oppression of its beliefs in a violent, angry, and vindictive God.

This is where you can come in. By deciding to actually talk about God more often, more openly, and with more people, you can play a role in bringing an awareness of the *true nature of Divinity* to others.

And you don't have to suddenly become a proselytizer to do it. Do you think that sharing with others that you are now choosing to have your own talks with God might cause a few eyes to blink—and a few new conversations to open? I promise you, it will.

Sometimes just telling others that you've read a book that you found fascinating, and in which they might be interested, can be all that is needed to stimulate the inquisitive nature of those who are open to deeper explorations of this deep subject.

Watch what happens when you say that the title of the book is *GodTalk*. Or *Conversations with God*. Observe your response to their reaction and, as time goes by, decide what you find to be the most effective way to ignite the interest of others in taking a new look at this whole subject.

A FEW WORDS OF GRATITUDE

*T*hank you for reading this book to its final page. The intent of this book has been, of course, to show you that you *can be*, and *have been*, having your own two-way communication with the Divine. I hope that some of the tools I've shared with you here will open you to vivid experiences of that reality.

It takes more than curiosity to continue exploring ways to integrate ideas and experiences that may be new to you into your daily life. It takes *commitment*—commitment to growth. And that is not a small thing. It requires intellectual bravery, personal determination, and spiritual openness. So whether you agree or disagree, resonate in full or in part—or fail to resonate at all—with what you found here, you have my admiration for your willingness to embark on the journey.

My admiration and my gratitude is sent, as well, to Sacred Stories Publishing for its wonderful work in producing the Common Sentience book series. This most unusual collection of texts reflects the publisher's own commitment to offering possibilities for growth to others, by sharing the personal experiences of many among us that could open doors which some people might not have ever given a serious thought to, until they saw the titles in this collection.

So, my thanks to publisher and reader alike.

MEET THE SACRED STORYTELLERS

REV. TIFFANY JEAN BARSOTTI, PH.D. is an internationally renowned medical intuitive, healer, researcher, and author of the book *The Biology of Transformation: The Physiology of Presence and Spiritual Transcendence.* healandthrive.com.

DEBORAH K. BATES is a harpist, singer, speaker, author, and Sacred U instructor. She is featured on radio and television and her music, presentations, and talks focus on connecting people to their divinity and nature. deborahkbates. bandcamp.com.

SUE BRYAN, PH.D. is a retired educator. Sue lives and writes in Santa Fe, New Mexico finding her connection with God in the beauty of the desert. inwardjourney2020.substack.com.

ANNE CEDERBERG is a naturalist and an artist, specializing in mystical nature experiences and the healing power of nature. Her mission is to help others see God in the natural world. ourmysticalnature.wordpress.com.

MARE CROMWELL is a Gaia mystic and high priestess, award-winning author, and healer. She has been told that her work with Mother Gaia is in the native prophecies. greatmotherlove.earth.

EMILY HINE is a technology, mental health, mindfulness, and compassion executive. She is author of the forthcoming book *Holy Sit: Learning to Sit, Stay, Heal, and Serve.* emilyhine.com.

DR. JULIE KRULL serves as a midwife for the evolution of consciousness, whole-systems transformation, and a whole worldview. She's a best-selling, Nautilus Award-winning author, speaker, and host of The Dr. Julie Show: All Things Connected. thedrjulieshow.com.

MARCIA LOWRY offers channeled energy healing and workshops through the Awakening Heart Center in Saint Paul. Sessions include Qigong sound, crystals, or EFT, to bring physical, spiritual, emotional, and ancestral healing. awakeningheartcenter.com.

SIOBHAN MAGUIRE is a sensitive empath who was diagnosed with cancer at age thirty-one and chose a completely holistic path to wellness, dedicating over 20 years to her work as a healer, coach, and therapist. healthyselftherapy. com.

JENNY MANNION healed seven years of diseases in three weeks and awakened to her purpose. She is an author, speaker, teacher, and healer inspiring self-love and manifesting the life we desire. jennymannion.com.

PAUL J. MILLS, PH.D. is a scientist, educator, and author of the Gold Nautilus Award winning book in science and cosmology, *Science, Being, & Becoming: The Spiritual Lives of Scientists.* pauljmills.com.

PAMELA D. NANCE has a master's degree in anthropology, researched the survival of consciousness after death, and has certifications in healing touch, past life regression, hypnotherapy, shamanism, and spiritual dowsing. pamelanance.com.

ANCA RADU is the mother of Ayan, a 7-year-old boy who survived an aggressive stage four cancer. She is a sociologist working as a full-time human resources manager and a shamanic practitioner.

BERNIE SIEGEL, M.D. is a leading teacher of the mind-body connection and well known for his New York Times bestselling book *Love, Medicine and Miracles*. Bernie is also the author of the novel *Three Men, Six Lives* and co-author with his grandson, Charlie Siegel, of *When You Realize How Perfect Everything Is*, a book of short writings and poetry. berniesiegelmd.com.

YAELLE SCHWARCZ is a creative heart, writer and soul art guide who combines her creative training and experience with her background as a massage therapist, workshop facilitator and speaker.

M. J. STANTON'S mission in life is to help the human condition by sharing her life experiences. That is why she writes and considers it her gift from God. livingwellministry.org.

AGUSTINA THORGILSSON is a licensed psychologist. Her vision is to help the world to a better place by showing people how to transcend even the most difficult life-experiences they can encounter and find peace. life-navigation. com.

DR. JANET SMITH WARFIELD is the founder of Planetary Peace, Power, and Prosperity Legacy Foundation, Inc., an educational foundation supporting those desiring peace, (em)power(ment) and prosperity in their lives. planetarypeacepowerandprosperity.org.

MEET THE AUTHOR

Neale Donald Walsch is the author of 40 books on contemporary spirituality and its practical application in everyday life. His titles include nine entries in the *Conversations with God* series, seven of which made the *NY Times* bestseller list. Book One remained on that list for 134 weeks. His works have been translated into 37 languages and have been read by millions of people around the world.

Learn more at nealedonaldwalsch.com.

MEET THE AUTHOR